Stand Against Bland

First published by BlackBird Books, an imprint of Jacana Media (Pty) Ltd, in 2019

10 Orange Street
Sunnyside
Auckland Park 2092
South Africa
+2711 628 3200
www.jacana.co.za

ISBN 978-1-928337-88-1

Cover design by Sechaba Kgalala
Editing by Nkhensani Manabe
Proofreading by Megan Mance
Set in Sabon 11/16.5pt
Printed by ABC Press
Job no. 0003637

See a complete list of BlackBird Books titles at blackbirdbooks.africa

Stand Against Bland

Sylvester Chauke

Founder and Chief Architect – DNA Brand Architects

For my dear parents, my super huzz – Tumelo, my bestie – Wilco, my tribe of all-stars and the incredible men and women who embraced my oddities and amplified my magic.

"Regardless of the space you are in, you must constantly be learning and looking for ways to improve and evolve. If you are not excellent where you are, you will think that excellence only rests elsewhere."

– Sylvester Chauke

CONTENTS

Part one

1.	What brings us here?	1
2.	Coming in awkward	3
3.	Sonically driven	9
4.	Success and the city	12
5.	Becoming Sylvester	15
6.	The little thief!	23
7.	The case of the late-night phone calls	27
8.	Self-acceptance	30
9.	Responsibility	43
10.	The gift my father gave me	45
11.	The struggle is real	49
12.	Turning off the lights	59
13.	The feeling of a place	61
14.	A vision of a home	74
15.	Self-care, self-respect	79
16.	Expressing yourself with style	83
17.	Not out of the woods yet	87
18.	Getting in there	89
19.	Straight shooting	94
20.	Let's unite for success	99
21.	A terrain of digital struggle	108
22.	Home is where the heart is	111
23.	A foot in the door	117

Part two

24. A first attempt   127
25. The bidding war   128
26. Greener pastures   133
27. Smaller, but bigger   138
28. Complicit in each other's success   143
29. Seedlings in a nursery   148
30. The spirit of change   150
31. How I run the business   152
32. Find your people!   162
33. Shut up and be grateful   164
34. What makes a leader   167
35. What drives you   170
36. Casting for crew   177
37. The skills of the future   180
38. The call of the bird   182
39. Work that wins friends   192
40. It's not just about the CV   201
41. Getting my African groove back   206
42. I was never ready   214
43. Now is my time   218
44. The Tao of DNA   223
45. This is living   227
46. The courage to self-actualise   230
47. A vision of the next reality   238

PART ONE

1

What brings us here?

IT MAY SEEM ODD FOR a man in his mid-thirties to be writing a memoir, but I've been lucky. Some fascinating experiences have blessed my life in a short time. I've built a 100% black-owned brand communications agency, which is home to some of the most incredible all-stars in the industry, from scratch. I established myself in my industry before deciding to start my own business, working in game-changing companies like Nando's and MTV, and at leading advertising agencies like FCB, Ogilvy and DDB. Through my work, I have gained recognition.

People have seemed interested in hearing about the lessons I've learned so far. I've been asked to address groups of professionals – young black people, especially. This book is a continuation of that. I'm turning my words and ideas into something physical. In a way, that is what my experience of business has been, too: turning ideas into something physical. This book shares some of those ideas, and also the stories of how those ideas were shaped.

This is a snapshot of me in mid-career: a youngish, black, gay man in a slowly transforming industry once dominated by white agencies. We're steering our agency through some challenging economic seas. But we're doing the thing! In the boardroom and on the floor of the agency, where the ideas are hatched and reared. It feels relevant.

I've by no means arrived, but, at the same time, I have so much to be grateful for. I am grateful to my God, to my family, and to the people I've worked with. What success I have achieved has been down to them. I thank them all for the lessons they've taught me. This story is theirs as much as mine. The knowledge is all of ours, to be shared.

2

Coming in awkward

How DID I COME TO work in brand communications? What led me to PR and advertising? Where did I get the idea that I might love this kind of work? How did I end up here?

When I grapple with these questions, in my mind I see the image of myself as a schoolkid in Soweto, just south of Johannesburg. At 12 years old, I had just started my high school career.

For my entire high school career, I was an inquisitive kid. But I was awkward at the same time. I knew I was different from my friends and my classmates, but I couldn't put a finger on what it was that set me apart. Some days, I had a curious feeling of watching myself from the outside. I feel that I am able to see myself – my speech, my actions, my mannerisms …

I'm not sure if this happens to anyone else and I find myself thinking: "This is weird. Why are you like this?"

I've grown up all over Soweto. I'm a conscious being. I came to myself a few years earlier. I understand that I am an agent in a life of my own, but, at the same time, I am a child of my family. My family has a strong, distinctive energy, but it's a humble energy, and that's how I express myself, and how I go about my life.

Now, it's a few years later. I'm in Orlando East – another part of Soweto, under the shadow of Orlando Stadium, and across the river from the famous Vilakazi Street, where the Mandela and Tutu families had their homes.

Those are but two of the hundreds of unique, powerful families that Soweto has been home to. Soweto produces strong people for export, as well as for local engagement. There is energy on the streets of Soweto. Energy and strong personalities. To get ahead, you need to have a strong energy of your own, and the knowledge of how to relate to the countless people and cultures that combine to make Soweto so unique. If you want to get ahead, you need to be noticed.

This doesn't mean being brash or abrasive, or getting in people's faces. No, there are many ways to be noticed, and many ways to achieve your goals. That's one thing we learn on the streets of Soweto. We learn about people. There's a way to relate to every type of person, and to get them to see you. To *really* see you; to notice, feel and respect you.

I think my people skills must chime with my personality and the attitude I have learned from my family. Ours is a more reserved approach to life. Cool, nurturing. On top of that family approach, I have this awkwardness of mine. This awkwardness that demands to be fed.

In time, I found ways to fill my time that would feed my soul and alleviate the awkwardness. I would go to dance classes or to Mama Jane's youth club around the corner. I preferred to stay off the streets, where my awkwardness was too obvious.

If I'm at dance class, at least I'm doing something. There, my awkwardness is not an embarrassing handicap – it's an asset. On stage, in the dance studio, at tap-dance lessons, I can be comfortable; I can amplify, express and celebrate my full personality. In those spaces, I am not different, or "less than"… I am just me!

Throughout my life, I've embraced that art of dance with gusto, and it's become my thing. I'm a dancer. We dancers express ourselves physically, we communicate through movement and gestures. We allow music to move through us, to find its own expression through our bodies. And as we do that, we enter the business of dance, the industry of entertainment.

That means practice, performance … and auditions.

Once I'd been introduced to dancing, I found I could express myself so easily – and I never got tired! I also found a new network of friends, and a community that loved my style. With my dance friends, I felt comfortable in my uniqueness. We would rehearse together, and when we thought we were good enough, we started going to auditions together. That is how I find myself at a particular audition in Rosebank, Johannesburg one afternoon in the 1990s.

I think I'm good enough – and the client does too. The next thing I know, I'm in a TV ad for a Family Planning programme! At this stage, I'm not even clear what the commercial is for, but I know it's going to run on TV, which is the pinnacle of coolness back in 1992.

Having passed my audition, I become part of the cast. I'm the talent! I have no inkling of the workings of the advertising industry, or even where my little dance routine fits in. But I'm excited, willing and able, and desperate to do well.

On the day of the shoot, I get myself to the Turbine Hall in Newtown, downtown Jozi, at 6.30am. Only when I approach the venue on foot from Bree taxi rank, do I realise what I've got myself into. This is a massive production! There are dozens of crew members, almost as many cast members ... This is the real deal – and I'm part of it. I've taken the day off school for this, and I'm here with the best in the business ...

Of course, it's just a normal day for everybody else on set. They're going about things as if they've done it all a hundred times before. I'm walking around with big eyes, trying not to get in anyone's way, but I can't get enough of this. I'm fascinated! I have my mental TV camera set on "record" the whole day.

A few weeks later, I see the ad on television, and all the processes that seemed so mysterious to me start to make sense. My goodness! So that's what we were doing! Sure, we were dancing, but that was all part of a film project that was bringing a script to life, and the point of it, the whole production, was communicating a marketing message to the whole country.

So this was advertising! Participating in a tiny part in the process just brought the entire industry to life for me. Now I could see it. From that day forward, I never looked at an advertisement in the same way again. That day at the Turbine Hall changed my life. It changed the way that I looked at any kind of business, or the marketing messages that they made use of. For the first time, I could understand the big picture.

I understood the context of my small role, but I also began to get an idea of where that TV commercial fitted into a broader business and brand communications strategy. In fact, the message of that commercial was politically sketchy – something about, "Don't have more kids than you can afford," while us kids danced around like cheerleaders for mass sterilisation ... But if you look past *that*, then that advert was a valuable experience for 12-year-old me. It made me realise that I'm a little person, but there's a role for me. I was even included in the pre-production briefings. I started to get a particular feeling. In the words of the song by the great Hugh Masekela, I was "part of a whole".

Somebody clearly liked what I was doing on that Family Planning ad, because a few weeks later I got a call-back for another TV commercial. This time it was for CNA, one of the biggest news agents in the country.

The Joburg dance scene around the turn of the millennium was a formative space for many aspirational young black kids. I met a number of people on that audition circuit who are still very much in the marketing industry today. If dance was how advertising found me, it would seem that I am not the only one!

But it's also fascinating to consider the path that life leads us on. My first great career breakthrough happened on the set of a dance production, but that doesn't mean that dance was my destiny. Oh no, my journey would have several surprises, detours and obstacles before I began to get an idea of my ultimate destination.

And so it is with many of us. Your big break is not necessarily what you're ultimately bound for. It's only the beginning. The key is to be open to that, to stay flexible and adaptable, ready to make the turns and direction changes that life might require. If I had remained chained to the idea of being a dancer, I might not have learned the thousands of lessons that the broader field of marketing had to teach me. I might be running a dance school in the Johannesburg inner city today. That might have been a fulfilling career, but I'm pretty happy that things didn't work out that way ...

———•———

You could say that advertising found me. I certainly didn't go looking for it. Once I discovered that milieu, I started asking the right questions. I wanted to understand how my dance contribution fitted into the broader picture. As I started wrapping my head around that – initially just so I could do my job as a dancer – I came to understand advertising, marketing and brand management. I never looked back.

Slowly, that awkward kid began to find a space where he belonged. Initially, I felt awkward, because I felt like I was different. And I *was* different. People related to me differently because I approached life in my own distinctive way. Some people even made sure that I knew I was different and it kinda sucked. I was inquisitive. But I remained determined to know more, to find things out. I continued to learn and to uncover fresh, new ways of making sense of the world.

3

Sonically driven

I CLEARLY REMEMBER THE day my big sister Thoko said to me, "Hey, what are you? Why do you like to speak English? You go to a township school, calm down!"

I was hilarious in those days: I loved speaking English! I sounded like a snob, even though I had barely even seen the inside of a Model C school, let alone been a pupil there. I am a product of the township education system – a proud matriculant of Nghunghunyane High.

There was a reason for speaking English as much as I could. In primary school, I had so many opportunities and found myself spending time around a lot of white kids and Model C-schooled black kids. I was always so stressed out in those situations. These kids expressed themselves so much better than I did, and I knew there was a gap. So, the young me thought, "If I want to get better, I better start speaking more English!"

I became deeply interested in white people's ways of speaking. Okay, I was more than interested: I was *obsessed* with being able to deliver my English the way it should sound! Over and above watching English news, I had a little tape recorder, and I would record myself speaking into it, and then play it back. I would read aloud from books and magazines, then listen back to my recordings and critique my accent.

"Mmm," I would think to myself, "That twang doesn't sound quite right."

I'm embarrassed to admit that I crafted my accent to perfection, back in the days when Model C accents on black kids were *the* thing. That speech clinic style of operating even infiltrated my school study methods. I would read my study notes into my tape recorder, then listen back to them to help me commit the information to memory. Really, I was operating on two levels: I was listening for the information, but I was also practising my delivery. Whatever subject knowledge I learned at school was learned in the accent of a Model C wannabe.

By the time I reached high school, I was recording all of my subject notes onto my TDK tapes. The system was practical, because it allowed me to find a private, focused space inside my headphones, away from distractions, where I could concentrate. Things reached the point where I struggled to internalise what I was reading if it was not read aloud. That was my method.

To this day, I like to read aloud, even when I'm alone. I'm no longer practising my accent, but I would be lying if I denied there was still a trace of Model C in there! To this day, I make copious voice notes. Whenever an idea hits me, I speak it into my phone for later actioning. It all started in our bedroom in Soweto, learning for my geography exams.

I'm not the only one in my family who is sonically driven. My dad loves music; playing records at full volume on the weekend was standard practice in our household. Growing up in that environment, I came to see music not just as entertainment, or even as a distraction, but as part of the fabric of life. Those vinyls of his – often Thomas Chauke and the Shinyori Sisters – also infiltrated my mind, along with my history studies, and my Randburg accent.

Today, I still like to work with music as my backdrop. The deepest house, the most obscure jazz, the most flamboyant pop standards and show tunes, you name it. I will still be able to focus through the music and put together the most compelling pitch document imaginable – especially when listening to my ultimate icon, Madonna. Music and I are fellow travellers, thanks to my dad.

When I was growing up, my father's taste in music was largely traditional, and often inspired by the work of our fellow clansman Dr Chauke. The good doctor has since been hailed as one of the founders of Tsonga electro, one of the fastest styles of electronic music on the planet. His earlier work was far more relaxed, though – but always with incredible messaging. You would learn so much from it. There was so much wisdom and truth in it. When my mother was arguing with my dad, she would say, "Wena, I wish that you could be more like the music that you listen to so often!"

We're a rather loud family. Perhaps because we had to shout to make ourselves heard over my dad's music! Besides that reason, we just like to laugh a lot.

My mother had three kids before she met my dad. One of them sadly passed away 15 years ago. From my parents' marriage, I am Child Number One. Then it's my younger brother and two sisters. Ours was a house of love, even if it was a loud, typical blended black family of brothers, sisters, and half-sisters. We might not have had much, but, for us kids, the key thing was we didn't *know* that we didn't have much!

11

4

Success and the City

THE SCENE OF MY BIG BREAK – the Family Planning ad that started all the trouble – was the Newtown precinct of Johannesburg's inner city. To this day, that part of town is very special to me. I'm a city person, despite having grown up on the streets of Soweto.

Soweto is home, but many of my formative experiences happened in downtown Joburg. Long before I landed that big TV ad, some of my fondest memories are of the times my mom would take me with her to her workplace in Johannesburg. There was the excitement of the double-decker bus trip into town. The way the bus would lean over, slightly top-heavy, when we rounded the corners to weave our way through the traffic. We made our way between the high-rise buildings to Mumzie's office in one particular skyscraper. From the lobby we made our way to the lifts and beyond …

My mother was an administrator at a company that made

contact lenses. Every morning, I would watch her leaving home in her smart street clothes. Seeing her at her work was such a treat. Once she got to the office, she would put on a spotless white laboratory coat and she was transformed.

We would take the lift to the first floor, where my mom would stride over to her desk, put down her handbag and settle herself in, before donning that magical lab coat of hers. As her work day began, she would start inspecting lenses, writing up reports and discussing matters with her colleagues. It all seemed so *important*, and I can't help thinking that some of that was thanks to her special lab coat.

———————

I believe in the power of clothing – the ability of our wardrobe to change the way people see us and the way we see ourselves. When my mother arrived at work and put on her lab coat, she changed in more ways than one. I must have taken that to heart, because today I express myself through my wardrobe. Professional, stylish, at leisure … I can put myself in that frame of mind by my fashion choices. I take the power of a well-chosen outfit seriously, because I've seen it at work. A two-piece suit not only gets you respect and opportunity, it also feels amazing, and puts you in the frame of mind for success.

Transformative fashion needn't be expensive, only *considered*. It should be consciously selected and combined with your other dress choices. I believe getting dressed should be as much a psychological routine as an aesthetic one. It's a process of choosing your garments, feeling the texture of the fabric, assessing the look, the balance of your ensemble. It's about finding the look that matches what you're going to be doing, showing that you mean business. Your outfit can be more than the sum of its elements. You make your outfit, but your outfit also makes you. The same way my mom's lab coat made her into a "scientist" all those years ago in downtown Johannesburg.

Meanwhile, I would be at a desk of my own, playing with the staples, being sent to make photocopies and creating works of art from the stock in the stationery cupboard. Just feeling the magic of that office, with my mom like an invincible technician, a glowing laboratory angel in her work outfit, was so special. That's the romance of the city.

———•—•———

Oh, the city is a special place. To a black kid from the townships on the outskirts of society, the city represents prosperity. To generations of South Africans, Johannesburg is indeed the City of Gold. The place where things happen. That is where you go when you want to become part of the economy, when you want to be included. The city is where you go when you want to see the world, because, for South Africans, the world is in Johannesburg. (Capetonians would give me the look of death right about now.)

In Johannesburg, you start to glimpse what our democratic nation's founding mothers and fathers imagined for our country. A democratic, non-racist, non-sexist and free society. My school was a black school, my society was a patriarchal one, a heteronormative place. But in the city, the shiny City of Gold, we can get an idea of what might be built to replace those environments. Here where my mother, in her office in her magic white coat, was treated as an equal.

5

Becoming Sylvester

I WAS BORN IN the year 1981. The day I came was a Friday. According to the popular fortune-telling rhyme, "Friday's child is loving and giving." I'll take that!

My very first little memories are of being treated as a bit of a special kid. I was the first boy to be born into my family for a long time, so I think that was why my mom and dad tended to spoil me a little. I felt showered with love, and I always seemed to have heaps of toys – just piles of them, crazy toys with special functions. I even remember a truck that had a telephone inside it. I was *that* kid.

By the time I was a teenager, that special treatment had given me a little bit of a confidence boost, that feeling of truly being loved, which each of us needs.

When I was four years old, my older sisters started going to school. The scheduled time for me to start my own schooldays was still a couple of years away, but I was curious. What was this "school" thing? I decided that I would accompany my sisters to the big First Day of School at the neighbourhood primary school, down the road from our house.

I walked with them to the school gates. Then I accompanied them through the gates. Then I came to see what the classroom looked like. Then I sat in on a class. Long story short, I decided I liked school and I stayed. I came back the next day, and I kept coming back every day after that. No one was going to tell me I couldn't go to school because I was only four years old. I was there, and my school career was up and running.

That's the story my mom tells me of how I started school. It appears I started so early that I don't really have any memory of the time before my first day. In all of my childhood memories, I was just always of school-going age!

I'm not sure if that would be possible today. I believe you are now required to be turning seven in Grade One. I think it's something to do with making sure that children are mature enough to handle the challenges of school and of socialising with peer groups. It seems I was a little ahead of that curve, and I wouldn't have it any other way.

I must have had a couple of brain cells to show for myself, because the teachers accepted that I would be able to grasp the material. My parents had no problem with it: my starting school meant there was one less child under their feet at home. They promptly organised me a uniform, and sent me off to school with my sisters.

At the beginning of my school days, I certainly never felt like a youthful prodigy or anything spectacular like that. Perhaps being younger than everyone else in my class made me a little shy, but I lacked confidence for a while. Still, the material wasn't particularly difficult to wrap my head around. This is Grade One and Two we're talking about!

I had begun developing the beginnings of a work ethic by that stage as well. I worked damn hard, and I made sure I was delivering. I established a standard of excellence. Every year, I would finish either top of the class, or second. When the report cards came out at the end of every semester that was the only question my parents wanted answered: was Sylvester top of his class, or second? Had my big rival Constance managed to beat me this year?

Township schooling provided me with all the knowledge I needed, as well as the people skills to get by in life.

I sailed through primary school and was similarly successful in high school. As I progressed through the grades, it came to be decision time. What path would I choose? Mr First-or-Second-In-Class, what'll it be? What career would suit me? As things happened, just as I was grappling with these issues, I scored my big break in the dance-themed TV ad scene.

That was a thing, but there was no chance of me going to study dance. It did not make sense. And what would my parents say? If we were going to be able to scrape the money together to fund a university place for me, it was going to be in a field that led to a recognised career. But what?

I may have been at the top of the class, but I wasn't firing out seven As every term. I wasn't quite doctor or advocate material, and I didn't feel like an academic either.

Intrigued by my little taste of the marketing field, I proposed to study a BA in marketing and communications. The bug had already bitten: I would have chosen advertising and communications no matter what! I had been hustling to get as much exposure to the industry as possible – going to career days, even attending orientation mornings at local colleges where I had no intention of studying – all just to find out a little more about my prospective career. I researched the subjects I would have to excel in at school in order to qualify, what the course might entail, what the elective subjects were.

Bit by bit, I assembled my knowledge about the marketing course. I was pretty clued up about my aspirational university career by the end of my penultimate year at school. One small obstacle remained: how to finance it. That registration fee is often the one thing that stands between you and your future.

I heard that the University of the Witwatersrand, the venerable old Johannesburg university, was a possible option if one wanted to study marketing. But on my adventures to the campus, the place didn't really grab me. Perhaps it was something about the elitist, ivy-lined walls, or the colonial legacy, or the rather substantial distances one had to walk across campus, but it felt like Wits wasn't quite for me.

Another option was the university then known as Rand Afrikaanse Universiteit, or RAU. As far as colonial legacies go, RAU was as culpable as any other established university. But there's no accounting for the capricious whims of our soul's intuition. To me, RAU felt good. It had a contemporary architectural feel, and it seemed that their sights were focused on the future more than the past.

If I cracked the nod from admissions, I would be among the first RAU student intakes that wasn't exclusively Afrikaans-speaking. I would be a pioneer of change!

The cohort before me had been forced to study in Afrikaans, whether they understood it or not. Change doesn't come all that fast in South Africa.

Luckily, some tendrils of English instruction had begun to take hold by the time I got there. The institution also had some progressive departments. The career centre, for instance, was amazing. One of their resident psychologists assessed me, conducted a fairly thorough interview, and confirmed that, yes, it seemed like I might do well in either the communications or marketing fields. Suitably encouraged, I began putting together the makings of a subject choice. Advertising was a must. Public relations, communication, sociology, philosophy … And why not a bit of French in there as well? Languages, just for good measure. We were learning to communicate, after all. It felt perfect.

I was going to be a student!

———•———

As it turned out, I ended up being particularly good at philosophy and sociology. In fact, by the end of my studies, I was being encouraged to follow postgraduate courses in those cerebral subjects. To this day, sociology appeals to me because of its cultural aspects. That's where I thrive: in understanding the human aspect of society, and how people express their humanity.

People. Groups of people. What makes an individual part of a group? How do people express their individuality while also identifying as part of a group? How does a group express the interests of individuals, while having a collective identity all of its own?

To operate in society in almost any capacity, you need a real understanding of culture and society. Understanding is one thing, and appreciation is another.

There are multiple ways of living, of expressing our values, of governing a nation, multiple ways of raising a country, multiple ways of growing up. I came to believe that socialisation does nothing incorrectly. There's no right or wrong. There are just people, and how they grow. My time at university gave me the tools to appreciate different perspectives and cultures – and I'm convinced my time growing up in Soweto taught me appreciation for cultural uniqueness.

University also exposed me to the literature, the centuries of work that humanity's greatest minds have created in considering the human condition and our social arrangements. There are as many theories about human societies as there are human societies! What does Marx say? Mill? Fanon? W.E.B. du Bois?

Funnily enough, that exposure to such a host of social theories didn't turn me into a slavish adherent of any of them. I certainly internalised many of the ideas, but I reserved judgement. I'm not a fundamentalist, and the more I learn about anything, the more I tend to develop a hybrid theory of my own. Having learned about democracy theory and the underpinnings of socialism, you could say my personal politics developed into a kind of democratic socialism, a fusion of theories that helps me make sense of the world.

I can appreciate what's good about one system, and what's good about another, and then synthesise them; even if ideologically, I'm combining oil and water.

But things don't always have to make sense for them to work. I grew up in Soweto, walking the streets with hustlers of all types, but then I would have to take a taxi to dance class in the suburbs of the North. Then I'd be inspired by a James Baldwin book that transported me to the streets of New York City. Then I would be in jazz dance class ... When your life is like that, you're bound to develop your own unique, hybrid perspective, and your own way of making sense of the world.

You come to appreciate the beauty of each of these worlds. You learn how to function and even excel in all of them. You learn the code-switching that will make you understood and win you trust in each context. You manage these worlds, to reconcile them in your own mind, so that they make sense. Any black person reading this will know what I'm talking about. Most of us who grew up in the townships, but have to work in the city, have learned to do this. We've taught ourselves how to switch languages, to switch dialects, cultural references. When to switch on and when to switch off.

It's a complex operating procedure, particularly in South Africa, with our half a dozen race groups, 11 official languages and more cultures and dialects than you could easily count. But, boy, it's fun. It's also one of the privileges of growing up in a place like Soweto. That exposure to so many rich cultures is precious. It starts off as a human instinct. We learn and adapt to every situation we find ourselves in. We learn to fit in. It's a little difficult to explain to someone who hasn't lived it. But we don't really learn culture so much as feel it. Perhaps that is the African approach: a bit less theory, a bit more feeling.

When you are lucky enough to come from an environment as culturally privileged as Soweto, and then later you find yourself in the city, you're well equipped. You realise that, "Hang on, these suburban kids with cell phones and nice clothes ... They're not any better than me." I learned early on to appreciate my own blessings, my own advantages, even if they weren't material advantages.

Being part of the dance scene meant taking two minibus taxis to get to rehearsals in Randpark Ridge, while my friends were being ferried around in SUVs. That is something you have to make peace with. The inconvenience of being poor. The cost. I think it was Steve Biko who noted that in South Africa, "it is expensive to be poor".

When you're exposed to such stark difference in lifestyles, at the back of your mind, in a quiet little corner of your heart, an awareness grows that you are definitely not the privileged one. Another realisation also grew within me, the teenage Sylvester at dance classes in the suburbs. It's not fair, I realised. It's not fair, and I didn't understand why it had to be like that. I still don't.

As I was coming to these realisations, I began to question my position.

"Why am I here?" I started to ask myself. "Why am I

struggling, when my friends are so well taken care of?"

I started to get a little upset. It's a slippery slope to go down, but I wanted to know: why was I born into this family instead of a better one? Why am I not being dropped off and picked up like everyone else in my dance class? Why do I feel so robbed?

There was a privilege differential in play, but I realised that I, too, was a lucky child, compared to some other people from my community. They weren't able to come to the suburbs to dance like I was. Even though I needed taxi fares and it took me two hours or more to get across the city to my classes, and then another two hours' travel to get home to Soweto in the dark, I needed to be grateful for even that. Even that opportunity is still a blessing for someone from a black family that isn't well off.

I had my own daily struggles – as many of us do – but we made it work. I often wonder how – but I am grateful for it.

6

The little thief!

Picture the scene.

I'm not yet in my teens, probably nine or 10 years old. I start sneaking money from my mother's purse. A R20 note here. R10 there. A random R5 coin in between. These are the days when Michael Jackson is the reigning King of Pop, so his look is huge! The look he started rocking after the *Thriller* album, when he started going on his world tours. The Dangerous tour – that military look. That look was my jam! I had to have it, and my love of things drove me to crime.

My parents laugh about it today, but I'm not proud of it. At my lowest ebb, I took R50 that was meant for important household purchases and went and permed my hair like Michael Jackson!

With the remainder of the money, I went to the supermarket and bought myself my favourite things: Ultra Mel, Romany

Creams, Tennis biscuits, Tempo chocolate, Fizzers ... there was also Mayo frozen yoghurt among my ill-gotten gains.

My criminal mind didn't stop there. I made sure I picked up a basic plastic packet from a roadside kip-kip stand on my way home, so it wasn't obvious that I'd been to an expensive store. That cover story would have worked very well, if I hadn't come home wearing an enormous, shiny Michael Jackson perm!

My parents were onto me immediately. I got the biggest hiding of my life – in my Michael Jackson perm.

"Where did the perm come from?" they asked. "Where did you get the money for that?"

I tried lying to cover my ass, telling them that my friend Eugene's mother had used me for the perm trial as she was practising to be a hairdresser. Parents are not stupid, though. The next Saturday, my mom woke me up at 6am in a mad panic.

"Oh, my son. Wake up! We need to go to visit Eugene's mom. We need to thank her for being so generous and giving you a beautiful perm!"

They had me. My deception had me painted into a corner. I had no alternative but to come clean about stealing the money.

"Where's the rest of the money?" my mom asked.

Just to make my actions that bit more evil and inexcusable, I had chosen to hide the rest of the money inside my copy of *The Children's Bible*.

"I just wanted to have nice things!" I sobbed to my mother in between spanks. "I just want to go out and have fun and entertain myself." Was that too much to ask?

— • —

For years afterwards, whenever I made demands, my mother would take the opportunity to remind me that I was a thief. It taught me such a lesson. After that admonition, I would just keep quiet and be grateful for what I did have.

I swore never to lose my way like that again. After my parents had put me in my place, I changed gears at school and started bringing home marks in the 80 and 90 per cent range. I became a good kid – not that I hadn't always been. I just became better at not succumbing to temptation. I had learned that you can make your dreams and aspirations real, but there are no shortcuts. I still liked things, and I wanted them, but I realised that by trying to get them easily, I was really just short-changing myself. The cost – in terms of work, effort and money – is part of what gives something its value.

I was heartbroken at having disappointed my parents, and I resolved to make it up to them, to win back their respect. It was time to work even harder. That was a watershed moment in my life. I had taken money that was meant for food, so the cost of my sweets and my perm had not been to me, but to my family. It was actually quite selfish of me, especially in a home with two parents trying their best to educate and feed their humble family. That lesson – the understanding of the real costs of our behaviour – has stayed with me.

I sometimes think that, when we choose not to pay the true cost of something, we are not simply getting ourselves a discount, or finding an easier way. Often, we are forcing someone else to pay on our behalf. The same principle applies to the most sophisticated forms of corruption, misappropriation of funds, fraud, theft, tax avoidance or profit shifting. We're not paying our way, and we expect someone else to take up the slack while we reap the benefits. Now that I understand this principle, any kind of unethical behaviour sits uncomfortably on my soul. All gains that come from unfair methods just don't seem legitimate to me. I would rather overcorrect, put in more work, go the extra mile, and win my success in that way.

I try to keep reminding myself of principles like these.

Temptation will keep rearing its head in new forms and contexts, as we make our way through life.

7

The case of the late-night phone calls

I WAS BLESSED TO BEGIN my career in advertising at one of South Africa's largest agencies, FCB Lindsay Smithers. I was able to find an internship there, so they must have seen some potential in me. But I was young, and I happened to have a boyfriend at the time, who had moved overseas.

In order to keep in touch, I had been calling him from the office phone. We missed each other desperately, and we would have the longest conversations. I made sure it was always late at night, because I figured, with Telkom "Callmore" Time, surely it couldn't be that expensive. How bad could it be?

Within a couple of weeks, a senior manager called me in about one rather lengthy phone call that had cost the company more than two hundred and fifty rand. That was a bunch of money in those days – it felt more like two thousand rand!

So, Romaine McKenzie called me into her office to discuss my late-night phone calls to my lover. It was just so embarrassing!

"Who are you calling in the UK?" she wanted to know. "So … It's not for work?"

She made it clear that I could not be doing that kind of thing with company facilities. I apologised profusely and explained that my boyfriend and I were really missing one another and I just had no other way to connect with my man. Romaine was quite understanding about my predicament, but she also explained that this was not the way to go about things. I would have to pay the company back for the calls.

So, for the next few months, the cost of those precious late-night calls to the UK came off my modest intern's salary. I was reminded every month-end of the true cost of misusing company assets, and of taking people for granted.

These were small things. Little life lessons I was fortunate enough to be taught at an early stage of my life. They've always been acutely embarrassing. In both The Case of the Late-Night Phone Calls and The Incident with the Perm, I had let myself down, as well as those who believed in me.

I was completely at fault, and guilty of misuse of the company's assets. But I had been blessed with an understanding manager who could see the human issues at the heart of what I had done. She gave me a chance to do better. Besides teaching me not to waste the company's money, this also taught me the value of compassion. As well as a kind of firm discipline, I had been shown understanding. I had slipped up, but I was a person, an imperfect human being trying to navigate this challenging adventure called life.

This lesson has come back to me later in my career, when the shoe has been on the other foot, when colleagues of mine and members of my teams have made mistakes. There have been many such occasions. After all, we humans are far from infallible. And whenever I find myself having to deal with these kinds of lapses and misdemeanours, I try to temper firm censure with understanding and an opportunity to make things right. If we can turn a disciplinary moment into a teaching moment, that's first prize.

I was issued with a formal warning and we had to come up with a repayment plan. But it was a massive wake-up call for me. I realised it was time for me to focus, to commit myself to my career with even more dedication – I had to change the way I behaved if I wanted to succeed. And that's exactly what I did.

The boyfriend? He is still in the UK. Things didn't work out between us romantically. Fate had put some distance between us, and we eventually left each other to go forth and learn our respective life lessons.

These lessons of mine have been massively important to me. In a country such as ours, having an accurate moral compass is a privilege. You're not going to learn lessons like these around every corner. For me, the worst thing that might have happened would have been for me to start being dishonest, and to get away with it. That might have set the tone for a life of unethical behaviour. Luckily, I was blessed to be discovered early on, and to have loving, caring people around me, who could help me back onto the right path, and assist in developing the ethical tools that serve me so well today.

It's good parenting, in a lot of ways. We inherit values from our parents and from our community, but we also need to develop some values of our own. Parents and elders can teach, correct and discipline until they're blue in the face, but if we don't take on board the lessons they're trying to share, there's only so much they can do. And if we come out of that learning period stubborn and defiant, without having learned anything … well, that's on *us*!

8

Self-acceptance

I CONSTANTLY HAD THIS feeling of being different. When I walked the streets, I felt awkward. People could see it, they could feel it too. They treated me differently, which only made me feel more awkward. The boys on the side of the road in Soweto … the kids at school … My parents and my family accepted me as I was, but even *they* knew there was something different about me.

Part of that was maybe the question around my sexual identity. Growing up, I didn't know that it could be such a big thing, because I had not had any kind of sexual awakening, and I still lacked the words to articulate that. But things did feel a bit bizarre. Even as I walked those streets, I would sometimes come out of my body and look down at myself, and see that … I'm looking funny because I'm just not like the other boys. I didn't feel like I belonged; I just didn't belong there.

I began to focus on finding myself, finding my way, and

building a life that makes sense to me. I have worked to get to a place where I can express myself honestly. I like to think that today I've fashioned a lifestyle where I no longer have to pretend. I fit in. I have embraced the awkward feeling. That awkward kid being sniggered at in the corridors at school, the boy who was disrespected on the street by the gents on the corner … that boy has found a place where he fits in and he's loved for exactly who he is. No, let me correct that. I haven't found a place where I fit in. I've *created* a place where I fit in. I've built a home for myself.

This has been a big theme in my life, because you have to somehow find a way to be able to deal with yourself and who you are – at home, with your family, in the streets and in your work life. This has to happen at the same time as you develop that moral compass and find the values that will guide you through life. We have to square those values with our identity. Self-knowledge is such a key part of life. You not only have to find a way of doing things, you have to feel comfortable with it.

Within this, there is a fascinating paradox. I am different, but I do belong. I have a right to be here. Even though I have built a life for myself that is unique to me, I am part of this society. As a human being, I deserve a seat at the table, and I also have a right to assert that. To demand it!

It's about more than the fact that it's okay to be different. Being different doesn't disqualify me from anything. If anything, I can enrich your society of traditions, conventions and conformity. Give me my seat at the table, and I'll show you the funnest dinner party you've ever had, darling!

My parents loved me unconditionally from the day I was born. They never made a big thing of my being different. They have always known how to handle me.

"Just let him do his thing" was their approach.

They gave me the space to do that, which was helpful. In the years before I was able to start building a life of my own, they

31

helped to create one. They never said, "Oh no, you can't leave the house wearing that. Go and change!"

I was allowed to go to dance classes, where I could express myself. They just let me do whatever felt natural to me. That was helpful because at least I never felt that I needed to be playing soccer!

That was a special gift that my parents gave me, and I hope that most parents are able to do that with their children. To accept them as they are, and to let them express themselves. But still. That thing of feeling awkward ...

Do I still feel awkward? I do, but I'm more comfortable with it now. In the end, I've made peace with it. I guess I've learned self-knowledge, and self-acceptance.

On my journey through the corporate maze, one of my job interviews brought the importance of self-knowledge into sharp relief.

I had been for an interview with the marketing director at a particular organisation, which had gone rather well. I got a very welcome call-back, but I was told, "You need to go to see the CEO. At his house."

That was good news, if a little daunting. But I am nothing if not ready to step up. On the day, I ran for the CEO's house with my pitch presentation. I am a firm believer in presenting during a meeting. If I have a proposal for you – such as the proposition that I would be a good person to hire for your company – I will present it formally, whether in a PowerPoint presentation, a video or a prepared pitch. I will craft my message in my own mind and then present it to you clearly, so that you can make the right decision: to work with me!

So anyway. I'm well prepared, I've got through the initial

interview, and I'm ready to meet the CEO. Well, I get there – to his private home – and the first question he asks me is:

"Are you gay?"

For a while there, time seemed to stand still. And then I said, "Yes. Yes, I am."

I was stunned, because questions about sexual orientation are seldom asked during job interviews. I'm not sure if they're even legal! Besides that, I was still young, and I had not quite come to terms with that part of myself. Perhaps people assumed things about me, but, in the work space, I had never before been asked directly whether I was gay. Let alone confirmed it.

But there it was.

We moved on to discussing other more relevant matters and, long story short, I ended up joining the company.

A few months later, when we had worked together on a number of projects and become friends, I asked my CEO about that interview. Why had he seen fit to ask me whether I was gay? He said to me, "I want to hire men and women who are strong, and who can stand up for who they are."

That man was looking for leaders. He was selecting a team of people he could trust. If he was going to have us around him, and working for the interests of his company, he needed to know that we were confident in who we were. And that we were prepared to stand up for that. After all, if someone isn't prepared to stand up for their own truth, how will they fight for yours?

"I gave you the job because you live your own truth," the man said.

Winning that interview changed me. It changed me because it gave me self-confidence. Someone had shown confidence in me.

———•———

I've worked at some respected companies. I've been able to start and successfully run a brand communications agency. I've been able to look after my family. I've won a lot of awards.

Some see me as possibly having some insights to share with young black people, young professionals. I get invited to host workshops, or to deliver keynote speeches. I get invited to a fair number of these things.

I'm often asked about the secret of my modest success. It's confidence.

And it's also understanding that I have to keep pushing. I appreciate that because I am good today it does not mean I will be good tomorrow. I have to keep myself sharp.

It certainly also has to do with building momentum in business. Having a track record of success leads to further success. But a lot of that is confidence. Success builds confidence, and that leads to further success. But it all has to start somewhere. Where does that first, initial spark of confidence come from? How do we start moving ahead? That first little fire of confidence and self-belief is kindled within us by the elders who guide us as children. They – the good ones among them – teach us that we are great. We are amazing just the way we are, and we have the right to express that. Not only *can* we be ourselves. We *must* be ourselves.

Many people struggle to express themselves at work, and that could be because they don't have the confidence to do so. They may not have the confidence to be who they really are – either because their company doesn't allow them to be that, or because something in their upbringing has undermined that confidence. Now they are left either trying to fit in or pretending to be something that they are not. And that is not the way to get the best out of someone. We are not all the same. We are each unique, with something unique to offer. I sometimes think, when we are forced, or we force ourselves, to replicate someone else, we make ourselves redundant, and we rob others of the magical uniqueness we have within us. It's so important that we stop this process happening. I believe we need to unlock all the talent, the magical creativity, the dreams and visions within each of us, by giving everyone the confidence to do it – their own way.

That interview experience was for a position at Nando's – South Africa's incredible, world-conquering food chain. That interview, and my confident response, was the moment when I took my awkward and I threw it away.

My awkward was no longer necessary. And what a huge relief that was. Sure, the awkwardness sometimes still rears its little head from time to time, but I just cast it aside. It no longer has power over me.

I now have confidence in my own awkwardness. Today, that awkwardness is a strength, an asset. It's one of my superpowers. If you also have awkwardness within you, consider that it could be the very thing that differentiates you. Far from being a flaw, awkwardness can be the source of your beauty. Your power.

Thinking back to that moment in my interview, I don't know where I got the guts to say that. To say yes, I am gay. I had never been in a similar position before. The man who asked me that question was Kevin Utian, then Nando's CEO.

He is a phenomenal man, and Nando's is a phenomenal company, which I was privileged to work for. As I've said, I'm not sure whether Kevin's interview technique would be acceptable in the contemporary political climate. It should not be, according to human resources best practice. One's sexual orientation is a private matter.

There were also very practical reasons for Kevin asking me whether I was gay. He is not blind, and he may have sensed that perhaps I am a bit "fruity". But he was looking for someone to fill a position where they would be dealing with a lot of fairly conservative restaurant owners. While calling on a team of staunch Afrikaans men, and trying to get them to buy into our marketing strategies, sooner or later I was going to have to deal with direct queries about my sexuality. He needed to check whether I would be able to deal with them.

I think the point Kevin was making was not that my being gay would be a problem, but that he needed a fully realised person at peace with themselves.

―――•――――

One day we were watching television as a family in the lounge. I must have been about 11 at the time. A flamboyant gay character came on television, an extremely dramatic, cross-dressing stereotype kind of character. And my mother said, *"Yo! Sylvester keo!"*

It was said in a jokey way. My family were laughing. But it was a complex statement. It forced me to think that perhaps this was the way people saw me. In some ways, that was the day that I started to come out. Of course, it took years for that process to unfold, but that day confirmed for me that I was different. People saw me as a figure of fun, which hurt more than you can imagine. I also got a sense that I was different, but it was okay.

"Sylvester keo!"

This is Sylvester.

That night I cried. And I cried so many nights after that. I could not believe that my mother had just compared me to this person. The way that she held me up as a caricature!

―――•――――

Today, I live as a gay, black professional. But I do that as a person from a generation where the only gay identities we were exposed to were these cross-dressing street characters in TV shows. Gay people feature in popular culture, but generally as shallow stereotypes. The drag queen, the choreographer, a stylist for a magazine, a make-up artist ... I fully support the right of gay people to follow any of those career paths, but that's not me.

In my career, I've found that I have to define my own identity. I am incredibly proud of the gay community, but we are so much more than designers, dancers and stylists. We are all of that, and then we are me: an agency owner in the marketing sector.

I'm lucky to be in a space where I have the freedom to be myself, but I understand that not everyone is that fortunate. In a patriarchal society, where heterosexual culture is the norm, it's that much harder for gay people to simply express ourselves as we are. A junior employee in an organisation that has always had the traditional macho hierarchy, for example, will have no incentive to come out, let alone to express themselves fully as a human being.

But everyone should have the right to be themselves. Culture can be its own worst enemy. Culture – in a society or an organisation – is meant to bind people together. But where it forces everybody to adhere to some fictitious common behaviours it divides people. Some of us won't fit in, and we won't feel welcome. Some of us will pretend, hiding our true selves. And that culture will be the poorer for it. It is robbing itself of the true expression of its people.

All people – no matter how they identify on the gender spectrum – want to feel accepted. We want to progress, but we want to do it on our own terms. That means not everybody needs to know that I'm gay. I need not make an announcement about my sexual orientation any more than the next person.

My only insights around this have come from my experience, which is limited. Not every gay professional will go through what I have, or experience it in the same way. But the ability to simply show yourself, and to be more of who you are, is so fundamental. My advice is just don't hide.

Sometimes we're the ones who hold ourselves back. Of course, the bigger tragedy is that often we do not find ourselves in safe spaces, where we will be accepted. But even then, we have a right to be who we are, wherever we are. People must get accustomed to seeing us. We're amazing. And if you want to succeed, be exactly that. Be amazing! Be so good at what you do that what you do in your spare time is not even an issue. There's a point where it's like, "Well, he's so clearly talented and so good at what he does that I couldn't be bothered to ask whether he's gay or not."

The better you are, the better you'll be accepted. In the Caucasian wide world, at least.

———•———

As a black teenager and a young adult, there's no point where you come out as gay while sitting at the kitchen table. You don't sit back and say, "I'm gay."

My mom yanked me out of the closet.

"When you and Smoo," – she was referring to Smanga, who I was dating at the time – "are fiddling in your bedroom, please use tissues to wipe yourselves instead of the towel."

I locked myself in my bedroom in shock. To make matters worse, Smoo came to see me that morning and my mom reiterated the tissue versus towel issue to him, too. He rushed into my room sweaty as hell.

There was no turning back, I was now "out" – just like that!

———•———

I think my mom always knew. She supported all my moves towards expressing myself, whether it was through my dancing, or in my fashion sense. People can pick up the nuances of each other's minds, and we don't always communicate in words.

Looking back, I realise that perhaps through my dance, and my style and all my awkward mannerisms, I was saying, "Look at me, Mama. I'm gay." And my mother, in turn, was supporting me in all my endeavours, never judging. Maybe teasing a little. Perhaps what she was saying was, "I know, my son. I love you."

Yes. I am a gay, black man, but I am so much more than that. I am a leader. I have to lead through the work that I do and the way I live my life. I let that speak for itself. Whether a person is gay or not is irrelevant. There is no need to marginalise ourselves by living up to stereotypes. Just be yourself. Do the work!

While my parents have accepted me, I understand that my being gay is still an issue for them. If they could pray it away, it would have been done a long time ago! But they've given me nothing but love and the support. I am their son. They don't want their son to be gay, necessarily. Perhaps there's a part of them that once wished for me to have a wife and many kids. But it's not going to happen like that. In fact I often tease them that I gave them three fur babies (Xiluva, Nyiko and Muschka) and that's quite special. Both of us have had to give up on such an expectation, of what we're supposed to become. Parents have their own dreams for us, of course, and sooner or later they have to give up on those visions for our lives.

I'm deeply grateful that I've been able to have a conversation with them about this. There was a time when I would never have imagined it would be possible. I'm sure there are thousands of black people in similar situations, living several lives. Where you act a certain way when you're outside the house, then you come home and you turn into a family man. The next thing, you're in a suit, and suddenly you're another person. Living like that is tricky. It's difficult to manage several identities at once. It carries a lot of a pain, and I'm not a doctor.

———•———

My awakening as a gay man happened gradually.

You could say I was a late bloomer. Throughout my high school career, I wasn't interested in any kind of dating issues. University, though, was when I started to venture online and meet more like-minded people. That opened up a new world for me. Even as I was going through that process, it still felt awkward; it was so foreign. The culture of online dating may be easy for some, but it didn't come easily for me. It is a culture outside of the mainstream, so I had a lot to learn. It evoked a particular feeling inside me. For the longest time, I just didn't quite know how to articulate that, to understand and express what it was.

Then, while at varsity, I got a part-time job. I worked at innovative retail company Verimark. I would staff their stands across Johannesburg – they operated as a small store within a store. At one point I was stationed at the Makro Woodmead store.

My co-worker and I would man the stand, make sure the products were invitingly displayed, help customers with queries and make sales through the course of the day. My colleague was a blue-eyed, white boy named JD. He's gay, and he was a bit more experienced about these things than I was. He had a more refined gaydar, perhaps. He spotted me for gay right off the bat.

There we were at Makro on a Saturday to serve our customers. We worked together, we laughed, and the day flew by. As we were packing up, JD asked me, "So, do you have a boyfriend?"

There was a beat in our conversation before I answered delicately that no, I did not have a boyfriend. I swiftly changed the topic and moved the conversation right along. I wasn't there to discuss my relationship status. But days afterwards, that question haunted me.

Eventually I phoned him and asked him about it.

"You wanted to know if I have a boyfriend," I asked him. "Do you think I'm gay?"

"Oh, come on," he replied. "You *know* you're gay. Of *course* you are!"

"No, I'm not!" I protested.

I was adamant I was not gay! In fact, I flew into a rage and started repeating some conservative rhetoric I'd learned in church about how I could not associate myself with gay people and I would not be able to see him outside work hours.

"Oh, come on," he said. "You need to get over yourself!" and he hung up.

But he had sown a seed within me. A seed of self-acceptance. Over the following weeks I started to come out of my shell, contemplating the idea that I may, in fact, be a gay person. I rolled the idea around in my mind, tried it on for size and found that perhaps it was my truth. Being gay might in fact be who I am. At the same time, I also got very scared, because when some people speak about "gay", it seems riddled with disease, promiscuity, the devil or hell. I was not happy with choosing a lifestyle that would carry with it such evil and negative sentiments. Hell no!

Verimark ran a roster system, so I would work with different co-workers each weekend. I didn't see JD for a couple of months, but eventually our rosters aligned, and we got to work together again. There must have been something different about me by that stage, because not long into our shift, JD piped up: "Oh, so you've decided that you're gonna be gay now?"

I was shocked at his temerity, but I didn't really have a comeback. I was coming into myself, and JD had helped me with that.

Complicating the issue for me, and for a lot of gay people in South Africa, I imagine, was that I came from a religious background. I had grown up Christian, and those values still lived within me. My Christian upbringing had helped give me many of my values as a human being. It had great meaning for me, and it still does. But according to church teachings, homosexuality is not right. It's a sin. By the letter of the church teachings, being gay is not compatible with being Christian.

I refused to throw out all of my Christian principles simply because I am the way I am. I have since been able to reconcile my moral values with my identity. I've come to realise that they are not incompatible. If both cultures and value systems are based on love, then they *can* live together.

JD was older than I was, and quite mature for his age. He was able to recognise what I was going through. He had probably worked through many of the same issues I was grappling with. We ended up becoming really good friends.

———•———

JD soon became my mentor on the Johannesburg gay scene, such as it was. It was a challenging time emotionally, and to crown it all I was kicked out of my then church because of my "impure" mind. JD was there for me; he helped me through. He took me out on my first visit to a gay club – StarDust, in downtown Johannesburg. We would go out to good restaurants, just show up where things were happening. He showed me around and helped me find the social scene and the support network that is so important when you're trying to learn self-acceptance.

9

Responsibility

MY LATE TEENS AND early twenties were an interesting time for me. I was trying to get through university, adjusting to the change from a township school to a state university. At the same time, I had this sexuality question coming up, which I had to square with my religious beliefs and my churchgoing. My academic performance was good. That only requires work, and I've never had a problem with hard work.

I remained cautiously optimistic. That approach of cautious optimism has served me well throughout my career. It keeps you honest. I've never been one for unbridled self-affirmation. When you feel untouchable is the time you're most likely to slip up and have a disappointment. University will teach you that. One successful semester test and you think you have this academic thing handled. Next semester? Thirty per cent for media law!

I had my moments of being cocky and overconfident, and

I was brought back down to earth with a proper bump. But I soon learnt to strike the right balance between my academics, my journey of self-discovery and my work commitments. I worked every weekend of my university career – Saturday and Sunday – because I had to.

Unlike many of my privileged peers at university, I had a responsibility to care for myself *and* for my family. This is a fundamental issue that anyone from a deprived or a working-class background will be familiar with. The business of making sure you have money for food and essentials never goes away. I was forever concerned about my parents and my siblings. My parents' fortunes at work would fluctuate, and I felt bound to contribute as much as I could to provide support.

I had responsibilities at home. But I fulfilled them with not a drop of bitterness, because I knew this was my time to contribute. My parents had done everything they could to get me to that point, and I will be forever grateful for that. The minute that I was old enough to earn, and to bring home some money, I did that gladly. Indeed, that's what all black children do.

10

The gift my father gave me

MY RELATIONSHIP WITH my parents is a curious one. We are full of love for one another, but at times we are a bit distant. This applies especially to my relationship with my father. That doesn't mean for one moment that he doesn't love me. When I was growing up, he went about his business, but he also knew when it was time to step up for his kids. One of the most significant moments of my life was the day my father set me off on my career path. It's a special day that I will never forget.

I was in my matric year, my final year of school, and the matter of what I would do after school was starting to come up in conversation. I had expressed interest in studying further, but there was no money for that. The only possible way for us to make it work would be to source funding from a financial institution. This is an obvious solution for someone from an affluent background, where getting a student loan, with your parents standing surety, is sometimes a formality. But for black people, who are generally excluded from the financial mainstream, loans are far from straightforward. With little generational wealth and no land to borrow against, we are basically relegated to the cash economy. This situation is changing slowly, but it persists, and this is what keeps us poor.

Imagine my father's situation. He was working, earning enough to just about put bread on the table, but here comes his son and says he wants to study at university! To his credit, my father took charge and did something about it.

One Saturday, towards the end of my matric year, my father took me to town, the two of us in our neatest outfits. It was a beautiful day. My father took me around with him, marching into the hallowed headquarters of South Africa's financial institutions and asking to speak to the bank manager. He introduced me as his son, and explained that I was interested in studying, would therefore be requiring a student loan, and how could we go about it.

This is an unexceptional day of business dealings in most parts of the world, but South Africans will understand the courage it takes for a working-class person to enter the world of finance and to demand their rights. We might not have had much money, but I was entitled to a future, and we were entitled to the funding that could make it a reality. So there we were, my dad and me in our smart clothes marching across downtown Joburg, from one bank to another. Standard Bank, FNB, Volkskas, Nedbank, United Bank, Allied Bank, you name it ... Sylvester and his dad were there, not begging for assistance, but politely and firmly enquiring about a student loan. These matters are not simple, but we were there to find out more, so could they please enlighten us and point us in the right direction?

By the end of the day, we had managed to secure a loan for R2 500, so that I could register at university. This was simply the first step. We had not yet reached the stage of financing the actual tuition of whatever course I would choose to study. But we had made a breakthrough. We had won the right to enter university. Of course, this should be the right of every young person, but the practicalities of life in a capitalist society are such that we needed to hustle. This was one of the most important gestures my father ever showed me, and I will never forget it.

For the first time, my dad was taking me out into the world. As I've said, my father was often otherwise occupied, and did not do much hands-on parenting. I had spent my high school years commuting alone to dance classes in the suburbs. I would arrive sweaty from public transport, to see my friends being dropped off by their parents, hopping out of their air-conditioned sedans, fresh and ready for class. I had come to accept that this was simply how life goes. I learned to deal with it.

But now, here was my dad, and he was doing that. He was there for me. We weren't in a smart car – we had taken a taxi to Gandhi Square from Soweto. But we were together. My father and me. We were walking together down Fox Street in downtown Joburg. Going into banks together. Sitting together in these offices discussing my future career. My father and me, together with these bank people. For a little bit, it felt like my father and me against the world. And we won! By the end of our brave adventure into corporate South Africa, we had secured my entry into one of the country's prestigious universities.

I am not from a very demonstrative "fetching and carrying" family. But there is love, even if it isn't expressed in so many words. My parents – and the parents of many black children – don't fetch and carry, they don't show up at 3pm to watch you play sports or perform your recital.

Black families are stretched at the best of times, so the time for ferrying to school and coming to watch sport is a luxury we do not have. We are forced to prioritise. We must determine very early on what the most important issues are. Every decision is make or break.

Prioritising is a special skill. I apply it daily in my business. I believe I learned a lot of it growing up in Soweto and watching my parents.

Black parents are working. They are rising at 4am to prepare lunch and then themselves embarking on hours-long work commutes to the other side of the city. There is simply no time for the demonstrative, expensive, time-consuming love that more affluent parents are able to afford. But there is love there. Love need not be performed. Love simply is.

But once in a while, when they do get the chance to open a door for you, black parents will grasp it with both hands. That is what my father did for me, that Saturday morning in the city. He opened a door for me. It is the best gift he ever gave me. That registration loan was my ticket to a better future. After that, anything became possible.

My father did that for me.

11

The struggle is real

LIFE CAN BE SO precarious for a black family, so I don't take my first step into university lightly. It was a foot in the door – and one that could so easily be denied again. I have had many such foot-in-the-door moments in my business life – in my entrepreneurial journey, especially. Each of these has been invaluable, and I'm grateful for every bit of assistance, every piece of advice that I've received. I have had a tough journey, and at times I haven't been sure whether I was going to make it. Those people giving me a foot in the door have been like angels to me. And I am nothing special.

Today, I sometimes find myself on the other side of the table, in a position to help others. In my business, I have had so many private chats in the boardroom with members of my staff. Young black people are so emotionally invested in their careers, because sometimes that is all that stands between their family and poverty. People break down in tears, their job can be that important to them.

"But there's nothing wrong!" I have to tell them. "You're doing well here! Your job isn't under any kind of threat."

"Am I doing well?" they respond. "I want to be. I want to be reminded. I want to be sure. I want to feel that I'm doing okay. I can't afford to lose this, because it's the only thing I have for myself."

My colleagues are so pleased to be praised and reassured. And I like nothing more than sharing praise and encouragement. But it does speak to the all-or-nothing life that we are sometimes forced to lead. These are tough economic times, so opportunities are precious. You cannot take them for granted, because you don't know when the next opportunity will come along.

This also affects our willingness to take risks. In an environment where up to 40 per cent of our workforce is unemployed, people are reluctant to give up a paying job on a risky prospect that may or may not pay off. That business risk is so much bigger when a job is not something you can just come back to if your business venture fails. That job is life and death. And it might not be there for you if you come back looking for it.

Managing a team of black people, and doing it with empathy, takes some emotional investment. It certainly helps to have come from the same place your colleagues are from. I find it gives me some understanding of someone else's journey. I know the struggle is real. It's *more* than real!

I believe being a black manager is not just about being a manager who is black. It's about managing people in an African way. That means using your understanding of our shared journey to manage in an effective but caring way.

A black person's struggle manifests in so many forms. For instance, someone who must commute for four hours every day from Daveyton to Bryanston and back cannot be scolded for being half an hour late to work (unless it is habitual). Ways must be found to accommodate her, and to make her most productive. This is such a fundamental brake on the South African economy. Our urban design is the same as it was during apartheid days, so the poor face the longest, most expensive commutes to get to their workplaces in the cities. I understand that changing this is a slow process, but come on! Hello, it's 20 years into the new millennium. Must my aunt still take three taxis – twice a day – to get to and from her work?

In the interim, while we wait for our leaders to transform our cities to serve the people who live in them, employers must find ways to accommodate this and to start fixing it. Today, my offices are in the north of Johannesburg. I try to help each of my staff to find accommodation in the suburbs near the office. I understand how much of a difference this can make to someone's life. It frees up two or three hours of every day, which they can not only put into their work with me, but into themselves. Into having a life!

I must be doing something right, because our company's staff turnover is pretty low compared to the norm in the communications industry! I'm also lucky enough to be spoiled with gifts, cards and letters from my team.

I'm not telling you this to prove what a love fest it is at our office. But the letters! Some of those letters are so emotionally powerful, they bring tears to my eyes. Again, with awe and wonder at what black people have to go through just to have a life.

One colleague wrote to me about how her parents had cashed in their entire retirement fund, and put it all into paying for her studies. She was so grateful, but at the same time she felt so much pressure not to let them down. Others tell stories of their parents moving out of their homes into a smaller house, to save money that they could invest in their children's education.

I know what this feels like, because my parents did exactly the same thing. They downgraded their lifestyle to help ensure a better life for us.

I was a child when this happened, and I remember feeling hurt and embarrassed. Why were we moving into a smaller house? What would people say? That kind of change can be traumatic. And with me being a liker of things, I refused to make peace with the idea that we were moving to a smaller house in a less nice part of Soweto.

The move was the result of a decision my mother took. It was supposed to be a temporary situation while we consolidated our financial position. But, ultimately, it didn't work out like that.

It all started with us upgrading our home. My mom and dad acquired a new, bigger home for us, and we moved with great fanfare into these pleasant new surroundings, in Meadowlands Zone 6. Part of this initial upward mobility was driven by my mother. She wanted us to live better, and she thought we would somehow find a way to cover the costs of the new home. We did. But that only lasted for a while.

Eventually, the reality sank in, and we struggled to afford the new house. Pretty soon, we ran out of money. We had to leave our new home, and we were living in a house even more modest than the one we had lived in originally; one we were not proud of.

These are struggles all black families face. Straining for better, but being pushed back down. We have experienced it all our lives, and that feeling never leaves you. Even in later life, when you have your own job, your own house, your own money … Even then, you are always aware of how tenuous it all is. How easily it can all be taken away from you. This is what black professionals feel, and these are the kind of issues you need to take into account when you're a black manager.

As a black child, when you grow up watching your parents

struggle, there is often an unspoken promise you make to yourself. That when you're grown, and you're earning, they will never again have to struggle like this. In your soul, you know, you are going to change this for the better. What they are investing in your upbringing will come back to them. You will make sure of that.

These are simply two of the issues we live with. That we want to do well for our family, to pay back what they have done for us. And on the other side, the feeling that no matter how hard we work, it can all be taken away. Just like that.

One of the achievements I'm most proud of is that I was able to see both of my sisters go to university. Of everything I've done – the industry recognition, the business successes, the jobs I've created – what made it all real to me, what confirmed that I had actually achieved something, was being able to send my sisters to university. That was me starting to pay back what my mom and dad had done by working their fingers to the bone for me. That was me paying back what my dad had done for me on that morning of interviews with bank managers.

Our responsibility to support our families is part of our value system, and we do it willingly. But we know that when we do it, we are paying for an exploitive system built by someone else. Should we have to? No. Do we do it? Yes.

We do it, until the day the people we help are able to support themselves, and to support others. We contribute what we can spare, pay what we can afford, to care for our families, and to pay for the education of our children. I understand this, and I'm always grateful for the opportunity, and for having the means to get it done.

There are limits to everything, though. Black professionals have to balance their own self-care with their responsibility to their extended families. There are limits to our emotional capacity to handle so much responsibility. And limitations on our financial capacity too. Sometimes it feels like there is no escape. We want to help. It's fundamentally unjust that our people are at such a generational disadvantage; that there is no wealth for us to fall back on. All we have is our salaries – if we're lucky enough to have that! There is no inheritance, no trust fund, no assets, no home that's been in the family for generations. All we have is what comes into our bank account every month. And from that, we are forced to make the most heartbreaking decisions. Will our aunt get money to see the doctor this month? Will our cousin get their school fees paid? Will our younger sister get to do the marketing course she so dreams of doing; the one that might get her a job in Joburg and start to lift her and her family out of poverty?

Will there be enough to afford all of this once we've paid off our car, our flat, our phone and our insurance? The answer to that is no. There will never be enough, and next month there will not be enough either. Each month, we will be forced to say no to something. It's easy saying no to a dinner for yourself. Or saying no to a new pair of work shoes. But to have to say no to a pair of school shoes for the girl your grandmother is helping to bring up? That pain cuts you deep.

Amidst all of this, this catch-22 financial trap that you were handed when you were born black, you have to make peace with yourself. You have to decide who gets help this month. You have to make the heartbreaking choice of who in your family you're going to help.

Prioritising is a special skill.

If you work hard, and you're lucky, you might be able to work yourself out of the trap. Thousands won't, but the fortunate ones among us will become successful enough to discharge our responsibilities, to pay for education, pay for a home for our parents, pay off debts, and reach a stage where we might spend money on ourselves. But throughout this process – which might take decades – we must love ourselves. We must treat ourselves with dignity and respect. We are each only one person, and there are limits to what we can do.

It's really our self-knowledge and self-awareness that has helped us achieve our successes. We need to protect that. We need to honour what we know about ourselves and provide for our own needs. We must nurture our own energy. We need to protect ourselves emotionally. Only if we are fully healthy – financially and emotionally – will we be able to take on those seemingly impossible responsibilities.

My second university semester came with the additional stress of that financial pressure at home. Christmas was coming. I wanted to get my sisters something nice. But before I could think about that, I still needed to finish paying off their school fees from my part-time salary. With the fees unpaid, they would not get their results, and they wouldn't be promoted to the next grade.

This was driving me to work overtime to earn a little extra, in between studying for exams. That led to me hardly being able to go home. My parents and my siblings would complain that they never saw me, which came with its own guilt. These were the early stages of learning about the economic trap. I had all these responsibilities, I felt guilty, I had no resources, no time, and I was tired, man. Life can take a lot out of you!

I knew that I had the responsibility to look after my family. Who else was going to do it? I was "the oldest", anyway. And the oldest ones must start helping out as soon as they're able.

Technically, I'm not the oldest. I'm the oldest of my mom and dad's children, but I took charge of fixing things. For me, the big thing was that I have a younger brother and two younger sisters to support. Today, I'm able to look back and think, wow, my sister graduated with a BSc Engineering degree, and I helped to make that happen. To have the opportunity to bring that to reality is the most amazing gift.

That little sister of mine is in the midst of her MBA now. Whenever a black child achieves highly, it's an achievement for all of us as black kids. Their success is our success. When we see a black child succeed, we know what sacrifices, commitment and dedication have gone into making that success real. How many aunts, uncles, brothers, sisters, gogos and tat'umkhulus have sacrificed so that one success could happen! That's why we succeed together, and we celebrate each other's successes as our own.

If all of us could only have this part sorted – these intergenerational obligations – if we could sort that out, we could fly. We would still be obliged to care for each other, and we would derive complete pleasure from doing it. But in the great race of life, we would at least get to start from the starting line, and not from 20 metres further back.

Investing in our families in this way also makes us emotionally invested. When you care materially, you care emotionally. Some of my friends tell me about the disappointment of supporting their family, sponsoring a niece through school, only to find out that she has become pregnant, or has got involved with drugs. These are the realities of life, but it's hard not to see it as human capital being wasted. This can lead to passionate interventions from family members, desperate to see their brothers and sisters succeeding in life. We can't judge people for the choices they make, but when we're so invested in their success, we can't help having an opinion.

This is a real challenge for us as black people. How do we navigate that?

At one point in my life, I carried a debilitating amount of

stress with me. I would feel my responsibilities physically, as an enormous weight on my shoulders. I would become exhausted, but sleep only very lightly, and then wake up in pain. My mind was constantly racing. I couldn't stop thinking about school, money, work, family ... What got me through it was prayer. The knowledge that there is a bigger power than me is a comfort. To know that someone is looking out for me, even while I am battling to look out for others. That gets me through.

The truth is, no one person can raise a family. There has to be many of us doing it together. Realising this has helped me see the true value of friendship and love. Finding commonalities with others, making friends ... it gives us energy. It lifts us up, giving us the support we need to be able to support others. Most of us black people are going through the same thing. All of us are spread ridiculously thin, trying to support extended networks of people with our finite material and spiritual resources. We know each other's struggle, which is why we are able to offer such incredible support.

My best relationships are with people who understand where I have come from. We're all struggling together, trying to fix generations of inequality. It's huge. Finding people who are connected to that, and knowing that I'm not alone, has helped me immeasurably. With these people by my side, I am assured that things are going to get better.

We are building an economy for the upliftment of black people, along with all South Africans. The economy can be that tool that helps to undo this inequality. I sometimes think that my business is a tool for that. I worked for a salary for many years, which gave me a finite set of resources for effecting change. Now, with my own business, I'm able to do so much more. I have found a more powerful way of hastening the change we need to unlock the unlimited potential of our black brothers and sisters. A salary can support one family, but a business, healthy and efficient, can help dozens. Hundreds of people win every payday. In a way, with our business, we're taking steps towards correcting inequality.

———•———

My business coach recently asked me, "If we took it all away, what would you do?"

He wanted to know if I would just go off to chill somewhere and relax. I struggled to come to an answer, but then I realised I could never do that. That guy chilling on the island eating crayfish, sipping a cocktail out of a coconut? That guy could never be me. What about purpose? What about the knowledge that everything I'm doing is aligned with my broader goals?

If financial returns were our only motivation, that island getaway might look attractive. But that's not why we're here. None of us is in it for ourselves. We're here to uplift the generations that come after us, and to live up to the faith and love of the generations that came before. That is purpose. That's why we do it. Legacy!

12

Turning off the lights

I HAVE A HABIT.

I like to work late, and often I'm the last one to leave the office. It's become one of my rituals when I close my computer for the day: I come out of my office, and I walk out onto the floor of the agency. I walk through the various workspaces in our offices, and I turn out the lights.

It's quite an emotional exercise for me. I walk from room to room flicking the switches and feeling darkness descend on this business that I've created. Finally, calm comes to this place that's been buzzing all day, this agency of black creatives and account managers and strategists and analysts. This bunch of brand communications all-stars! It's not an enormous agency – I can cover the length of the whole office in about 60 paces. That doesn't matter. I turn the lights off, and I think, "Hmm. I did it, right here."

———•———

I'm so grateful. When I look at photos of myself as a toddler, I feel sorry for that little kid. If he only knew. I can understand every little pinprick of how that little boy feels. I can see the awkwardness. But I also know what lies ahead for that little boy. And that is something incredible, a life so thrilling. He's going to travel right across Africa, activating campaigns in the most celebrated venues in the world. He's going to win awards on the global stage, he's going to be part of building a transformed industry and creating a better country.

The journey is going to be a fascinating one for that little kid. That human experience is going to blow his mind. I know, because I've lived it!

13

The feeling of a place

MY FATHER WORKED in a big civil engineering construction business as a clerk. My mom was an administrator for an optician. They're still married. That is an achievement.

They have a typical relationship in that it evolves.

How long have they been together? Forty years? And what makes it more magical is that they don't completely "get" each other. At times, my mom might complain to me about some trouble she is having with my father, and I'll say, "Why is it a big thing now? You've been complaining about it for decades!"

I grew up feeling that our family could do better. Not that we were simply entitled to better living. But that we can serve together and make a better life for ourselves. I have brought that feeling with me into my working life. The idea that we can be better by serving.

My message to young people is to dream.

I understand that sometimes your dreams are all you have. When I was young, and we were living in the newly established homes referred to as "DiNew House", it was a painful experience. My mom had worked incredibly hard for us to be there, but over time, the cost of running that household became a bit too much for us. We moved to Snake Park, Dobsonville. That was a significant downgrade, and I was uncomfortable with it. I understood that we were only staying there in the interim, while we were consolidating, but I hated it still.

I was in my preteens at the time, and that was a weird shift. As a youngster, you don't know the details of why you are moving, and why to that particular area. Moving to a brand new house in Meadowlands Zone 6 had been my mother's way of proving that we could do it. We could be upwardly mobile. We just needed to seize the moment and do it.

———•———

If only it were so easy. We were trying to build something more for our family, but it didn't work out. And then, the next thing I knew, we were moving to other, far less salubrious accommodations. The upward mobility became a downward slide.

Not being able to do anything to assist in that moment is a profoundly helpless experience. But once I'd rallied, I decided I would no longer just accept my life. I would not live passively. I have agency, and I am an actor in my own show. When I saw the less impressive location that we were downgrading to, I announced that I would *not* be staying there.

I believe those moves – which were instigated by my mom – were a stunt of sorts, to try to get my dad to really wake up, to see what was possible. I think she hoped that moving to a more upscale location would encourage my father to try harder, to also start driving success for us. It was a tight financial proposition from the outset. The idea was that my mother's salary would cover our daily living expenses – mainly food and consumables – and that my father's income would go toward the house. It worked for a while, but then we reached the limits of what our finite resources could finance, and we had to retreat. We had to pull back from our dream.

To me, Snake Park seemed one step up from a squatter camp. It was a "site and service" kind of location where the government and the developers had provided stands, with sewage, electricity and sanitation services, and then the new residents could build their own homes, plugging them into those service assets.

You can obtain a title deed in these situations, so it would be unfair to call Snake Park an informal settlement. But for a self-conscious preteen, it was a serious comedown. When I go back to visit now, I see that the area has really improved. The trees are more established, which makes a difference, and the houses are now made of brick, where the first shelters were built using corrugated iron, or zinc sheeting. But being among the first families to move into an area is actually quite a jarring experience. There were two rooms in the house. Two. When I first saw the place, I thought my parents were still just discussing the possibility of moving there, theoretically. It's not really going to happen. But then my mother goes and buys the place!

Funnily enough, the rest of my family didn't have such a problem with the house. There were parts they even liked about it. But I was hurt by this comedown, and I felt it deeply.

"Oh my God!" I thought. "This is what we have become! Living under zinc sheets! On such a tiny plot!"

Our next door neighbour's wall was a metre from our back door. The floors were uneven, sloping into the street. The foundations were shallow, and everything felt temporary and precarious – like our lives.

I decided I was not going to stay there.

Fortunately, my older sister had a place of her own in another part of Soweto, and she was able to put me up. So that was my course of action: going to live with my sister.

It felt like my mom had been trying to shock my dad into action, but it wasn't working. She was second-guessing his reaction. But people are unpredictable, they seldom react the way you expect them to. My dad was not moved to action. He understood that this was our new home, and that's where we were going to stay for the foreseeable future. For me, this was nothing short of disastrous.

I moved into my sister's house, staying there with her and her husband. I would go to visit my family on weekends, to get my pocket money, and to share some family hugs.

I was there often enough to feel what it was like to live in that neighbourhood, in Snake Park. With us being part of the first wave of residents, it was a fairly dusty township. Until it rained! Then it became a completely different ball game. When it rains in that kind of house, suddenly, it's dripping everywhere, water flowing under the doors, flooding the floors, everybody scrambling to lift off the floor any possessions that might suffer water and mud damage ... You don't want to be around when it rains. And I did what I could to get out of that place. To this day, every time it rains, I think about those families living in houses like that. Today, I live in the northern suburbs of Johannesburg. I know that I've come up. But I cannot forget where I've come from. In fact, it breaks my heart that so many of my people live under these conditions. It's not fair.

That heritage is nothing theoretical. It's real. Every single time it rains, your possessions are in danger. That's another reason you'll never hear me talking about the "good old days". It pains me to think of those days. Today, I might be sleeping in my cosy bed when a Johannesburg thunderstorm hits. I might wake up immediately, or I might become plagued by dreams of that house in Snake Park. It's wet, the ceiling is dripping, water coming under the doors. Us pulling up the rugs, moving the furniture to save it from the rain …

The feeling of that place has never left me, even though I didn't spend much time there. It's a painful experience for me.

That house in Snake Park taught me that no one plans for their lives to be that way, but it happens. We had been almost bourgie, for a black family. We lived in a bonded house. And then – wham! – we found ourselves in an environment where we were just desperately trying to survive. Fighting to live. I have so much compassionate understanding for people who find themselves in that situation. You cannot judge them. No one plans it that way, it just happens. Decisions are made, but you cannot foresee how things will work out.

Living in difficult environments has taught me the importance of spatial identity. We are shaped by the spaces we live and work in. Our mindset, our mood, our attitude … all of it is affected by the places we occupy. And we do not always get to choose the spaces we live in. In fact, our spaces are usually determined for us. By our income group, our culture, our profession. And from there, our spaces shape us further. They shape us and also our families.

I understand the importance of having a positive space. Where I can, I try to assist people in finding and creating their own spaces. It's important to me where my co-workers live. It's important that my team members live comfortably. I quiz them, from time to time. "Where are you staying?" I'll ask.

Is it a house? A townhouse? A flat? A four-room in the township? These are not arbitrary options. They will shape you. That's why I always try to pay people well enough that they can live around the area where we work. Then, live that lifestyle if they choose to. Most of us at the agency, 90 per cent of us, live in the area.

Why was I embarrassed to live in Snake Park? Mainly, I think it was a case of wanting to do better. I had dreams, I aspired. Even when I was in Orlando East, I had always wanted to do better. The thought that one day we would move to somewhere better would keep me going. But I could not accept the idea of moving somewhere worse, of going *down* in the world. That goes against the essence of aspiration – the idea that we will improve our circumstances.

In my business, I tell my teams that if you have the opportunity to change something, change it! Do that for yourself, for your family. You have to, because I believe that you cannot live without really adding value to your surroundings. One of the basics of life is growth, the idea that we evolve, that we are becoming. If our circumstances are getting worse … is that even living? It becomes very difficult to live life in that way.

There were six of us living in that house in Snake Park. I remained a visitor, with my "country residence" at my sister's house. My family were there, and I was with my sister. They were there all through the establishment of the area. The years went by, trees grew. The trees grew! But did our prospects grow? That was my concern. Anyway, instead of being a temporary arrangement, Snake Park become a way of life. It became the norm. At the same time, on the other hand, my oldest sister was really giving me an incredible opportunity. I got to live with her and her husband and two other children they were raising. They looked after us well and it was really amazing – another type of family environment.

In hindsight, the fact that my parents even allowed me to do that is quite something. It says a lot about my parents, and a lot about my younger self, that I was basically able to move out of home at the age of 12. But these kinds of pragmatic living arrangements are not unknown in black culture. Luckily, my sister was there for me, and provided an option when I really could not see any other way forward. I see it as progressive parenting by my parents that I was able to say, "I'd like to go to stay with my sister's family."

That I was able to say that, and indeed for it to happen, shows that my parents really listened to what I had to say. I was getting real respect as an individual. I already had agency at that young age.

———•———

Towards the end of my school career, I was hustling, already with half an eye on going to university after school. I was selling things around the township, getting odd jobs, doing whatever I could. I knew that just to be able to register would be a challenge for me. The rest of it … if I could get myself a bursary, and work part time, we would manage it. This is what I was telling myself at the age of 15, already plotting my vision of a future that a township child was not supposed to have. But I was not going to be a prisoner of my circumstances. I needed to ensure that I got there, that I made my dreams reality. As a small child, your environment is given to you. But after a certain age, it's on you. You control your destiny. For me, that age was 16.

I moved out of our house, but in some ways, I never did. Other black families will understand what I mean. By the time I was at university, I had found an apartment in Auckland Park, near the campus. But even living there, at the back of my mind I was always going to remember: "I'm doing all of this with my family."

That's how it's been for me. My life has been about earning a better life for my family, whether we are living in the same house or not.

Moving out of the parental home might sound like a great

step for personal freedom, but it's not. It's lonely, and tough. You have some companionship, but only your parents can provide that deep nurturing love and support that we need as children. I missed that.

I journal a lot. Reading back through my journals, I realise that at times I really felt the absence of my mother and my father in my life.

"I just wish that I could see them," I would write. "But I'm working."

I needed to do the things.

I was physically nearby – Auckland Park is only about 10km from Soweto – but by the time I was at university, every minute of my spare time was applied to my part-time work. That was what I needed to do – spending time with my family was a luxury. Of course, this is not unique to me: many of us are forced to move away from our homes in order to support ourselves and our families. But it speaks to a great generational trauma not often spoken about: because of our economic and social circumstances, even the love of our parents – family love – becomes a luxury for us. For me, it started happening when I was 12 years old, but for children in some families, it can happen from birth. The baby raised by her grandmother in the rural areas, while her mother goes to work in the city. The child sent away from her parents to attend school in another town. The parent forced to leave the home where their family has lived for generations, in order to sell their labour in some dehumanising environment, to live as a single person even though they have a family. This is what the shape of our country's economy means for us.

The physical distance from my family was negligible, but it was difficult to do something as simple as going home for the weekend. That trip home had a cost – in travel expenses, as well as the opportunity cost of work that I needed to do. I needed to be earning. Taking the weekend off meant no money for me. And so it tended not to happen. I missed my family, and I wept some nights, in the room of my shared apartment, after I'd come home from my evening shift at the call centre. On weekends, I worked for Verimark, doing marketing, merchandising and sales at Makro and various shopping centres around Gauteng.

I might be making it sound like mind-numbing work, but working in those environments really sustained me, and I will always be grateful for what those jobs allowed me to achieve. It was decent pay, and those companies looked after us well. With my earnings, I was able to start building an independent life for myself, away from the family. I was able to buy a fridge, for the modest meals I was living off. My food was just real basics like noodles, bread, mince, cheese and achaar ....

And all through this time, I'm constantly thinking about what I need to do next. How am I going to do it? How do I move myself to the next stage? How do I help my family manage their situation? This is how many of us live.

My part-time work was invaluable in that it showed me that I was able to make a material difference. Week by week, I was able to send money to my mom and my family. To help them buy chicken pieces for dinner; my little contribution. It's not like I was supporting them at that stage. The work I was doing was just a supplement, a top-up to the money that my mother, my father, my sister and her husband were bringing in. But it did give me a sense of responsibility, and that was empowering. It was important for me to be able to assist them, to do my bit.

When you're working to help your family, achieving at work is not just a pleasant reward, an acknowledgement of your contribution. It's real. Every bit of recognition might lead to a promotion, or a raise, which has practical implications for your family. Another five per cent on your salary could help you pay the phone bill, or the water and lights, or a week's groceries.

These are the real incentives for workplace performance, and I realised that from the very beginning. Around the time I started getting acknowledged at work, my job started getting better, the part-time, weekend gigs started getting more frequent, and I had more to contribute.

After university, when I began work as an intern at FCB, I certainly gained a sense of accomplishment, but looking back, the main feeling I remember having is that I was starting to feel really useful. I was thinking, okay, now is my time to step up, and I'm managing to do that. I wasn't just earning pocket money, after all. Maybe the amounts we're talking about would be pocket money to some other people, just some extra cash to pay for a weekend of going out to restaurants or partying. But for a black child who has grown up listening to his mother talking about her issues and the impossible task of trying to make "not enough money" stretch to cover "too many problems", that little something extra means an opportunity to contribute meaningfully at home.

The traditional, western paradigm that might prevail in certain economies is that the parents will spend their working lives supporting their children, then they will retire and, around the same time, the children will come into their own in their careers and start supporting the parents in their dotage. That is the theory, but, in South Africa, the reality is somewhat messier. From birth, we scramble to survive, to cover the family expenses, and we develop a hustler's mindset from early on. We grow up listening to our mothers talk about their issues over the kitchen table. We learn that everyone must contribute, no matter how old they are. That contribution might be through earning, or through contributing our labour, doing chores that have value.

The challenges are real. Will we have enough food? How will we pay school fees? I need money for transport, for kids' clothes … It's the same old story. You don't need to explain this to any black person. Most of our families are in this situation. And so, as we start to earn our own income, we don't have to be told about where money is needed. We instinctively *know* what to do. Some of us even develop a sixth sense for that. It's not always part of black culture to directly ask for money. So, you can help your people by anticipating, by noticing. When you come to visit the family, you walk into the house, and you know exactly what to look at. At my parents' house I open the kitchen cabinets. I open the fridge. I see what's there, and I know what is needed. That is precious, because then I know how I can help.

I come back with the things they need, which allows us to move forward without getting them to a stage where they have to ask for help. It's challenging for any parent to have to ask their child for money, or for material help. They have their needs, but they also feel that you have your own thing going, and they don't want to bother you. They tend to keep quiet about their needs, so part of helping is doing the work of finding out what is needed. It's not good enough to just say, "Well, they haven't asked for anything, so they probably don't need help."

I was grateful that my family seldom asked me directly for help, but at the same time I knew that didn't absolve me from my responsibility to contribute. No parent will tell their child, "We need this from you because we paid for you to go to school. Now it's your turn."

That might be another of the social contracts between the generations, but it is seldom expressed in so many words. I believe it shows how well my family raised me that I knew the responsibility I had, as a big brother, to help make sure that my parents and my siblings were completely okay.

I started feeling like I was adding value, giving my mom a little money once in a while. But the financial needs were always there. And the accepted path of school, university, work is simply not going to cover those needs soon enough. The earning needs to start here and now, wherever you find yourself. There is no time to wait three years, until you graduate, before you start allocating some of your salary towards covering family needs. The contributing starts early on, and we need to find ways of earning where we can. In the same way that I started my school career sooner than I was strictly supposed to, I began my work career *way* early.

Even while I was doing all my part-time jobs, I had my eye on the advertising industry. I knew that was where I wanted to be. I began doing research, finding out what the industry offered. How did one enter the sector? What did they have in place to let young talent into the space? My research revealed that FCB, one of the venerable, established South African advertising agencies, offered an internship programme. I decided that was going to be my entry point. That would be how I got in.

I was only in the second year of my marketing and communications studies when I applied for that internship. There was no time to sit around. I went to see them, I applied, I poured my heart and soul into that application and I won them over. There was still the small matter of me being a full-time student, but a young hustler doesn't let that stop him. I negotiated an arrangement where I would attend university every Monday, Tuesday and Thursday evening. I would scramble out of work at 5:20 in the evening and make my way across town to attend night classes. I was also able to hold on to my call centre job, which I would fit in after I finished classes at RAU. I was part of the workforce long before I stopped being a student. Life was busy. Fortunately, we have energy when we're young. I remember feeling tired, but I was able to get by without much sleep in those days.

I was also fuelled by desperation. I needed to get ahead, to start making a difference. My family was still living in Snake Park, and I was not happy with that – never mind that I was slightly embarrassed by it. Now, I was in a place where I could start *doing* something about it. I sensed that here, with this income from two or three jobs, I was getting myself into a position where I could improve matters. I could be part of moving the family out of that house that had been a source of pain for me. That house!

So, I was juggling. I was juggling my parents, my family, as well as my university commitments, my weekend work, my internship at FCB and my call centre work in the evenings.

The Sylvester project began evolving.

14

A vision of a home

It's ALMOST IMPOSSIBLE to run two parallel lives at the same time. It took a couple of months for me to figure out what to do, but gradually the solution revealed itself. There have been a number of proud moments in my life, and this was one of the proudest. At some point over this period, I had been able to start bringing in a consistent income. The work was consistent enough to allow me to walk into a bank, and to apply for a home loan. As I walked out of the bank after getting that home loan, I remember thinking to myself, "I'm going to change my family's lives."

I had a vision for that house, a picture in my mind. In the same way that I knew what groceries we needed at home, I knew what kind of house we had to have for my family. It needed three bedrooms and two bathrooms, with an en suite for my mother. A double garage and a nice spacious kitchen. Then, it had to have a garden for some greenery after the dust of Snake Park. After what felt like months and months of battle, I was able to find just such a place in Protea North. Some people call it "The Northern Suburbs of Soweto".

The family knew that I was house-hunting, and I had even brought them along to a Sunday show-house day to get an idea of what was available. The house we got to see was a good deal better than the house in Snake Park. They were already like, "Hey! This is great! We can move in here!"

But I knew that we deserved better than that. I also wanted to prove a point, that I could actually *do* this. I eventually identified a house, went into the bank, applied for the loan, signed off on the payments and secured the property. Once I'd achieved that, I drove to the old family home – by this stage I'd been able to get myself a little pink Fiat Uno hatchback. I headed down to Snake Park and picked up my family. Then we drove over to the new house. That drive – with my mother and my two sisters – that was the day that everything changed!

That was the gift I was able to give them. It was so precious to me that I was able to do that. Across South Africa, in townships and suburbs all around the country, there are black children doing that for their parents. Helping them to find a better home, to move up in the world. Helping us transcend the limitations that our iniquitous system would impose on us. Helping our families get to the next stage. We really are quite magical!

At that point, I was working about five jobs. Soon, my mother stopped working, and my dad did too. In a sense, it was all on me. Life was challenging, but it was such an amazing thing to be able to do that. That day I showed my mom her new home was one of my proudest moments.

Since that experience, I have known that I can achieve almost anything I set my mind to. I know I can achieve what I want because that was a huge leap. At that stage I was 21 or 22 years old, but I had taken a quantum leap into a new level of independence and self-confidence. I'd got it done! We still needed some furniture, but we didn't worry about that. We moved in. The family had a new house, and that was all that mattered. We had elevated our lives, and it was such a privilege that we were able to do that with my assistance.

Today, my mom calls me at least every week. She will tell me, "Oh, my son. Do you know where I'm calling you from? I'm in the bath!"

Those phone calls give me such a sense of fulfilment. It reminds me that I have been able to help people. That sense of accomplishment doesn't come from bigging yourself up. It comes from being able to help, from serving. That gives you confidence. The knowledge that, little me, I can make a difference. And if you can achieve that, if you can help to lift your family out of difficult circumstances into something better, then just imagine what else you can do!

I am nothing special. I am just a black child doing what he needs to do for his people – and there are thousands, millions of others like me. But we shouldn't lose sight of what we are achieving for our families. That achievement of raising someone's living standards is massive. It's huge! And so many of us are doing it every month. We need to remind ourselves how impressive that is, and take encouragement from it. We must use that sense of accomplishment to power further achievements – for our families, for our people and for ourselves.

Truth be told, there is no bigger gift to yourself than to be able to make a real difference in someone else's life. It may sound like it helps the recipients, but the real beneficiaries are those doing the helping. What a privilege it is!

Those achievements are part of what made me. I walked away a changed man. Today, if I were to lose my business, my car, my house and all of my assets, nobody will be able to take away the fact that I was able to buy that house. Today it's all paid off, and it still stands. We were able to do that. That might be one of my greatest achievements.

Many friends of mine have done similar things. All of us have, at some point, helped to move our families up. And all of us are so supremely grateful to have been able to do that. It's such a gift to be able to repay to others what was done for you. It is never stated in so many words, but I felt such an obligation to have to do something to elevate my family. And being able to discharge that obligation is such a pleasure.

Whenever I get an opportunity to speak to audiences, whether it's at an entrepreneurial event, or an initiative to inspire and energise young people, I remind them that it's possible. Whatever you're dreaming of, it's possible. Every day, we work miracles for our families, so there is nothing that can stop us doing similar things in our careers or in our businesses. That inspires me: that black people are achieving so much with so little. Helping to change their fortunes with just a few small opportunities, an awareness of what needs to be done, and a determination to succeed. Many of us black professionals are in that position. Today I am an employer, so I am in a role where I can facilitate that, to help my colleagues help their people. These are the facts of being a black business person. It's such a special position to be in.

Many families from other communities are blessed to not have to do this, this work of rising out of poverty. There are also a few black families with that kind of generational wealth and ability, but the majority of us are still trying to move on from an extremely basic quality of life. Many of us are the first in our families to get a tertiary education, or to own a car or a house. We are trailblazers for our people. To this day, I find myself going into spaces where my family have never been before. Travelling internationally, speaking and meeting people in new spaces, making deals … And every time I do that, I tell myself, I am doing this so that it will be easier for those who come after me.

When my younger sisters started earning, they were able to support the cause in the new house for my mother. They were able to take over the reins from me and begin making their own contributions. I must say, that felt pretty special.

The black children of today are in a different space, because some progress has already been made by the generations that came before. However slowly, our people have been moving up. This talks to the vitally important progress in development and transformation that has been made in our country. We need more progress, though. We need more people in the middle classes. We need to free ourselves of these generational obligations.

We need to get to a stage where we can buy ourselves a new pair of jeans without feeling guilty that the money should rather be going towards food for our nieces and nephews somewhere in Limpopo. We need to be able to travel to the UK for a year or two, to experience life and to have adventures. We need to be able to go backpacking if that is what we feel we need to do. Many of us have had these opportunities, and have had to turn them down because of our generational responsibilities. What have we sacrificed of ourselves in doing that?

Perhaps we'll never know.

15

Self-care, self-respect

DESPITE THE DEFINITE soul-enriching benefits of helping our people, the things we can do for ourselves also have value. Personal growth is what gives you the experience to achieve more. Starting a business that will have exponential benefits for others begins with developing yourself – through study, work, travel and experiences. Those give you confidence and a sense of strength. This is not a theoretical conversation! Successful business people don't win the lotto. They develop themselves and they apply their learnings to their lives and their undertakings.

I went through formal channels to start my business. I didn't get a sweetheart loan, I didn't have a gambling hustle. I didn't sell drugs. I just worked. There wasn't even a big, magical lucky break. I sought out opportunities and I worked to take them. Sure, there were moments when I was in the right place at the right time. We all need some luck, but I also worked the hard yards. I did the work – in my family life, my professional life, and in my current incarnation as a business owner. I went through the process. I also know that everything I have gone through was necessary to make me the person I am today. It has helped shape my work ethic, my sense of purpose, my leadership style, my vibe ... My experiences have given me maturity, and they give me the energy, knowledge and confidence to keep going.

I have a great, rather diverse circle of friends. Many of them I was at university with. I have Chinese friends. I have a couple of white, English-speaking friends too. Speaking to my Chinese friends is interesting, because we seem to have a similar understanding of family responsibility. We have the idea of taking an active part in building success for your extended family. My white friends seem to have a different perspective. I sense they have a greater sense of individualism, that they have been equipped to be self-sufficient. To "stand on their own two feet". I don't judge that set of values, but it is different. It comes from another cultural viewpoint.

We may have come from a similar university environment, but my friends and I will still have different perspectives on life. I came through varsity in a state of always having less money than my peers. It was another manifestation of my experience at dance classes, where I had to transport myself via taxis from Soweto to Randpark Ridge, while my friends were dropped off by their moms. At university, I could socialise, but I would always have less money. At the bar, I would nurse a Coke while my friends drank the place dry. They might order burgers, while I would rather have a cheese-and-tomato sandwich when I got back home.

I might even have had some money on me at those times, but I also had this deep, ingrained sense that it would be irresponsible to go big. That feeling may or may not be valid, but it stops you from living your best life. An instant coffee and a Snackwich for dinner in your flat. Deciding that, no, you won't be joining your friends for movies ... That was my experience as a young person, and you know what? It's fine. It gave me character, a kind of humility but a certain amount of self-respect.

Those days of doing without, of getting by with a little bit less, are what helped me to buy that house for my parents. Culturally, my father remains the man of the house. I have just been the engine that has helped to power the household. Today, that has earned me some respect in our home. My dad looks at me in a certain way. I feel that I have earned his respect, and that is priceless.

Getting here from the days when I was embarrassed to go home to Snake Park, when I used to lie to my friends and tell them that I stayed in the fabulous houses on the far side, has been an interesting journey. During my high school years, I wasn't happy. I was uncomfortable. I think I carried some shame with me, about my circumstances. I didn't want people to feel sorry for me. That was the last thing I wanted, because ... Don't feel sorry for me.

I just didn't want people to know. If I got a lift home from the dance school with the mother of a friend of mine, I would ask to be dropped off a long way from home. There near the nice houses. And I would walk a kilometre or two to our house.

"Can we drop you off at your house?" people would ask.

"No, it's okay," I would say. "It's okay."

Many of us are familiar with that response. "No, it's okay."

It comes from a place of pride, but it's a good pride. It's a pride that will not be reliant on others. It's a pride that will lift itself up by its own bootstraps. A pride that will be fine. A pride that refuses to have other people feel sorry for them. From that pride comes self-respect. I am a strong, resourceful person, it says. I do not need your pity. I will make it. Thank you for your offer, but I will make it on my own steam.

In terms of the next step for a young, working black man, the idea of starting a business was not always there. Most professionals will consider it at some time. But, for me, it could only happen when I didn't have any debt. Thank goodness I was able to pay off my car so that by the time I was in a position to go out on my own, the only risk I was taking was sacrificing my salary. I had taken care of my responsibilities to my family. Now I was ready to take some business risks.

I have always been one to live within my means. Even once my business had built up some momentum, I lived in a two-bedroom townhouse complex across the road from the office. Friends would say, "I would have imagined you in a bigger, grander home. Shouldn't you have moved up the LSM ladder?"

My reply was that, no, I was starting a business. In fact, I thought my small apartment was pretty awesome. The last thing I needed to be doing was moving into an upscale mansion!

My career in business hasn't involved anything too sophisticated, or required savvy financial management skills. It's just the same basic principles that have served me so well since I was a kid hustling to pay tuition. Just control what you're spending, and – like every black person – keep running, keep earning, and save, save, save!

16

Expressing yourself with style

A SERIOUS CHALLENGE TO the concept of saving for success is that in the city there are just so many opportunities to spend money. If you feel peckish, you can go for lunch. If you don't watch out, before you know it, you can drop R1 000 on a meal for two. In the evenings, what with wine and starters and desserts, you can spend double that! *Or* you can bring a skhaftin of last night's stew and pay nothing for lunch.

After a few of these out-of-control restaurant outings, my partner and I decided that even our special occasion date nights would have to be modest affairs. We had a wedding to plan, and every thousand rand saved was a thousand rand that could go towards the wedding. It certainly doesn't hurt to have a target, something real that you're saving towards, to keep you motivated.

I once had a boss who had no problem spending six or eight grand on a bottle of wine. I have no issue with enjoying the finer things in life. But I would leave him to make those purchases and be more than satisfied with a small taste of that bottle of imported wine. Good for you, you connoisseur, but I'll just have a taste. In the circles I move in, I tend to interact with people who are spenders, but that's not how I operate. I like to treat myself once in a while. I might buy something lovely for my mother or get myself a birthday present. But that's it. I've learned that what is really valuable is not the big ticket possessions, but experiences. Life is nothing but a series of experiences, and if your income allows you to access special experiences, your life will be richer. It's about what you live through, and what you get out of it, as opposed to building a vast collection of objects that you can hold on to.

I like to think I have a well-developed sense of style. I can recognise what is fashionable and what kinds of garments will work for me, but even that needn't cost a lot of money. Style is really about combining garments creatively and with class. But you can pick up clothes incredibly affordably and put together a killer look for next to nothing. I was very pleased to be named the best-dressed man of the year by GQ magazine, and let me tell you, that doesn't necessarily mean money.

I avoid being called a fashionista. I dislike that description. It's not me. But I do believe we should be able to express ourselves through the way we dress and to have the style vocabulary to do that. If I want to look fun, or professional, or creative, I know which clothes are going to help me do that. It's a good skill for everyone to cultivate – to build a wardrobe that caters to all the various looks you're going to require in your life. And then to have fun with it, put together different combinations. That is how I look at it. I certainly don't spend tens of thousands of rands on random clothing.

I got much of my fashion sense from my parents. My mother is stylish, and my dad too. He was always in a suit when I was growing up. My dad has suits for days! At least a dozen suits in the wardrobe, and then an impeccable selection of shoes and ties to pair them with. He taught me about looking your best, dressing with style, and doing it with quality. You can put together some really stylish pieces by shopping wisely. You just have to be able to recognise them. Fashion does not have to be money related. The converse is also true – you can spend a bunch of money and still not look good. So, educate yourself.

A good friend of mine worked as a fashion stylist and he dresses incredibly well, but he doesn't spend much at all. He picks up random pieces from the same chain stores we all shop at. He just knows how to mix them. Fashion sense is about being selective, having an eye for the right garment and the vision to know how you might combine it with the other pieces in your wardrobe. It's possible to put together an ensemble from odd bits and pieces and look like a million dollars! It's all about how you put it together. The whole is indeed more than the sum of its parts.

Style also speaks to pride, self-respect and quality. The way you dress reflects your state of mind. When you respect yourself, your look should reflect that. This is also a black thing. We are not often blessed with financial resources, but we can put together a look that rocks like nobody's business!

In our office, you would be hard pressed to tell who lives better. My office is a predominantly black environment and, from looking at the way people dress, you would be unable to tell who lives in an RDP house in the township, and who lives in a mansion. Our cleaning lady who looks after our offices will arrive at work wearing stylish winter boots, a scarf and a jacket. Killing it! And then she will change into her cleaning outfit and get to work vacuuming the office. It's an established theme among black people. My mom was the same, and my dad too. As a black person, you learn that when you walk out of the house, you need to look impeccable. Even if you're travelling in a minibus taxi, you dress in a way that demands respect. No one should be able to tell whether you live in a squatter camp or a gated community.

It's an important part of who we are. We are always looking our best, putting our best foot forward. You don't wear your environment. Black pride is there. We express it in the way we carry ourselves and in the way we dress. For us, it says, "I'm transcending my situation". I am a person. I'm poor, but I have pride in myself and I make sure I look my best. It's the same in the way we look after our homes. In the townships, no matter how small a plot might be, you can guarantee that the stoep will be shining red like the setting sun. The tiles in the kitchen will gleam. The windows will glisten.

That four-roomed house in the township might be in better shape than an apartment in a townhouse complex in the suburbs. The townhouse will be cleaned by someone who is paid to do it. The house in the township is cleaned with pride. The suburban house is a place cleaned by a housekeeper. The four-room RDP house is a statement of who we are. You learn this pretty early on, as a black kid. You learn to clean your room. You get up in the morning and you put your affairs in order. You've got to be neat. You put your few little toys and things away carefully.

When I wash the dishes, my ritual is that after I've put away the last of the crockery, I wipe the sink and I clean it with Jik. I bleach that thing! Because that's what my mom does! That's what my sisters have always done. We present ourselves and our environment the best way we possibly can.

17

Not out of the woods yet

I MIGHT HAVE MOVED the family out of Snake Park, but my sisters still had to go to school there. I would wake up at the crack of dawn and drop my siblings off in my little Uno. Then I would have to travel across town to Sandton, to the agency where I worked. Anyone who's been to Johannesburg knows that the traffic can be murderous. I was up with the birds but I was still trapped in traffic with the masses; it would often drive me to tears. My commute was going to take me three hours, whether I woke up at 4am, 5am or 6am! This is another part of the black professional's burden: long commutes that often lead to being late for work. That kind of chronic lateness affects your standing at the company. You look unprofessional, but sometimes it's almost impossible to be on time.

I had just managed to do this amazing thing in moving my family into a better house. But it soon became clear that we were not out of the woods yet. There is a whole lot more to upward mobility than just signing a 20-year bond and moving house. There is still the schooling and the work, and the commute and the entire apartheid spatial-planning legacy that is directly aimed at keeping black people oppressed. As a society, we have not yet managed to undo that legacy, and our family certainly was not exempt once we'd moved to Protea North. It took until the beginning of the next year for me to get my younger sisters enrolled in a school nearer to the new house. That made my commute a bit more manageable, and I could get to work without being late every day. That felt like I was finally cresting a hill. I started coming out the other side. Life was getting better, but the levels of tenacity it took to get there were monumental. I'm sure many of us have lived that too.

Businesses are ostensibly equal opportunity enterprises, so every employee is treated the same. At my first agency job, we were all expected to be in the office by 8.30am, whether we had to travel from Sandown, or from Orange Farm. Getting in late can be a brutal experience in some offices. There is some public shame to it, as you trudge to your desk with everybody else already well underway with their work day. Some of your colleagues might understand your challenges, they might feel your pain, but you are left exposed every morning. The late one.

No excuse is good enough in those circumstances. You know how long your work commute takes is the implication. You should leave earlier. I refused to make excuses for myself. I realised that no one owed me anything, least of all sympathy about my morning work trip. But part of me wished it didn't have to be that way. The company had shown faith in me, in choosing me, and I didn't want to let them down.

18

Getting in there

THE MINUTE THE CALL for internship applications had come out, I had been determined to crack it. This was the culmination of years of awareness. I knew I was destined to work in advertising, and this was my long-awaited opportunity. I was not about to let the chance slip. Getting an internship was in fact a course requirement at the university.

Of all the agencies we could apply to, FCB was my first choice. It was an agency with a deep history in South Africa, where it was formerly known as Lindsay-Smithers. The tasks on which we would be judged were group assignments, and I was fortunate to have in my group a girl named Kesebone. Kese was awesome and, best of all, she had a car. This was like gold. Not all students had cars in those days – especially not black girls!

The two of us started brainstorming ideas, but then decided to take matters into our own hands and go in to the agency personally. Submitting assignments and hoping for the best just seemed like too much of a lottery for us. We determined that the best course of action was to go to FCB and tell them why they needed us working at their agency.

We got into Kese's white Citi Golf, drove across town and just showed up at the agency. The next thing we knew, we were being ushered upstairs and introduced to some of the leading lights of the company. We ended up in the office of the highly incredible Qingqile "Wing-wing" Mdlulwa and the respected Brett Morris, who would eventually rise to become CEO of the company.

We clearly made enough of an impression on the team, because we pretty much barged into the agency and never left. We understood that the internship application was basically a pitch, and that the only way to be noticed among the dozens of applicants was to do something remarkable. We submitted our assignment in a pizza box, with some suitably pizza-themed copy about "Get a slice of new young talent!", "We'll be topping the rankings!", and "Open! To meet the upper crust of creative talent!" It got their attention.

Then, once we had our foot in the door, we made sure they didn't want us to leave! I took every opportunity to make coffee for every single one of my bosses. Every client, every supplier that entered the agency, I was there ready to put a pot of coffee on. I would do anything to be helpful. Put petrol in your car? Fetch lunch? Go to the shops? Send me! Send me!

That internship programme was supposed to last for 12 months, but I had only been at the agency for six months when they offered me a full-time job. Throughout that time, I tried to give everything I could. I would go beyond the call of duty wherever I got the chance. That agency breakthrough represented hope for me. It was my future, because I knew this industry was where I was destined to make my career. I knew

I was starting to succeed when the various divisions in the company started squabbling over where I should begin formal employment. The client services department was interested, as was the strategy department. It's good to be wanted, and it was a welcome confidence boost for a new kid in the industry.

I had spent a month or two at the various divisions, and it gave me such a thrill to know that I had made a good impression on all of them. It was just great to be in demand. My instinct to serve was serving me well. Eventually, I decided to join client service, because I thought it would allow me to get some insights into strategy and some complementary skills – and quite honestly, because it meant I would be dealing with people.

———•———

The urge to serve just emanates out of me. I'm not sure whether it was taught, or whether it is simply one of my natural character traits, but I do love serving. I could be travelling with colleagues, and if we get into the business lounge at the airport, the first thing I'll do is get behind the bar and start serving drinks or pouring coffees. If I'm working with a client, I'll make sure I serve them too. Drink? A snack? How is the aircon for you? There's no cynicism to it, and there shouldn't be. After all, the essential principle of agency work is that we are helping clients to achieve more with their business. It's an extension of that same service principle.

As the agency, you're not simply there to get the work, do the work, and get paid. The fundamental sentiment is one of service. Being of service is how we add value to the work we do. That service might involve providing advice or consulting services, creative development, data analysis or strategic planning. You will do well in an ad agency if you're a servant by nature. Luckily for me, serving is one of the things that I love to do. Whether you're the business director, or the head of client service, a service ethic should be what drives your delivery.

When I joined Nando's as the national marketing manager, I learned that this same principle of humility and service was embedded in the best companies. Within my first fortnight in senior management I was working at a Nando's restaurant, taking orders and working the grill, and carrying our customers' chicken meals to their tables. This not only taught us how our company worked from top to bottom, it also reinforced our service ethic, and ensured we had the humility it takes to put the customer first, in everything we did. Whether you're in the boardroom or in the stores, your role is to sell and to give customers what they want. I really understand this approach. Too often, senior management seem to feel they are above the nitty-gritty business of operations. To that, I say, "Hello! You are here to sell just like everybody else. So calm the hell down!"

Humility is necessary. You need it in business, to remain in touch with the country that keeps you going. Without an understanding of our people, you're not going to get far.

———•———

I'm certainly no saint. I have a long way to go in my development as a person, and as a professional. But I keep learning, and I never decide that I know all there is to know about my industry. I keep humility and that service ethic in my arsenal at all times. Just recently, I was on our office telephone switchboard, learning how our phone system works. It was a gap in my knowledge that I needed to remedy. I sat at the DNA reception desk for about an hour manning the phones. I put out a tweet saying, "I'm on reception duty today. If you want to speak to me, give us a call."

There is no better way to gain an understanding of how

things work in your business; no better way than doing the work yourself. That holds true from answering the phone to making coffee to managing a department. This is another reason we work our way up in an industry – so that we get a holistic understanding of where everything fits in, and the challenges of every position. No role is any more important than the others. Everyone is vital. Imagine what would happen if a client can't get through to you on the switchboard!

As CEO and business owner, I need to understand how everything works in my business. If I can't make a client a cup of coffee when we're having an after-hours meeting, I look helpless, and it makes it seem as if our business systems are flawed. I make a point of learning all of those skills. If you come in to DNA and you feel like a cookie, I can go and get you one. I know where we keep the office keys. I know how much we pay for coffee. I understand the importance of every role in our company. And it's fundamental that everyone's role should get equal respect.

19

Straight shooting

I DON'T PLAY GAMES in business. Finding the right clients, partners, suppliers and people is a vital part of how I work. I insist on honesty, and I actually get incredible anxiety when I can't be completely honest with someone. I don't enjoy even the slightest evasiveness or someone trying to skirt issues. If we're not honest with each other, then what are we really doing? I firmly believe that straight shooting is the key to doing business effectively. We say what we do, and we do what we say. If an approach is not going to work, we need to be able to tell each other. You have the hard conversations and you move on.

Don't say "Yes, I'll come back to you" if you don't intend to. Don't lie to me. No one ever succeeded in the long term by using deception. I'm aware that in some corners of the economy integrity is seen as a "nice to have", but for me it's non-negotiable. Being shifty with your clients or your colleagues is not sustainable. Sooner or later, the whole truth will emerge, and then the entire house of cards will come crashing down. Business success demands a culture of sincerity and truth. It all speaks to our common humanity. Not being sincere with someone implies you don't really respect them, and respect is critical. Even more so, if we're in the business of communication. To communicate effectively, we have to respect each other as people. Otherwise, what are we doing here!

Real communication is intuitive. It transcends age, culture and gender. If we start from a place of mutual respect and compassion, communication will come naturally. Only if you are obfuscating and being evasive will you have to second-guess yourself. That's when communication becomes difficult – when there is deception. I refuse to play that game.

I try to be a good judge of good people. That may have a lot to do with growing up in Soweto. Coming from a township like that really arms you with an awareness of so many languages and cultures. It helps you understand how to address someone, and to really understand their situation, to be able to see deeper into their souls, beyond the basic matter of the words they use. Language is about so much more than words, and to really be able to communicate, we must learn all of each other's languages, we must be able to gauge the nuances of each other's character. A multicultural environment is invaluable for helping us learn these skills. South Africa is blessed in this sense, with our 11 official languages and numerous nations living alongside each other. There is still a need for far greater integration, but there are places where we live together and learn to really "see" each other as people.

This allows us to communicate in more than one dimension. Being chained to language as a medium of communication can blind us to many other realities. There are things we will not see. We'll miss the nuances of what people are telling us, and misunderstand how best we can communicate with them. My upbringing may have helped, but I do think I have a gift for seeing the full picture of what is being communicated – and what is not being communicated.

Agency people will recognise how important the subtleties of communication can be. "It's not what's being said, it's what's not being said" is something I've heard many times. A client email might be more abrupt than usual. The senior manager might sit in a particular way during a meeting. They might use a slightly odd turn of phrase. There are many signs we need to be able to pick up and respond to appropriately.

Another invaluable business skill is being able to understand the essence of a message. That's what has helped us to solve so many client briefs. In a 100-page briefing document, what is the main problem? Can we sum up in one sentence what the client has taken an hour to articulate using a PowerPoint presentation, a video and speeches by four board members? If we can, then we'll be well on our way to getting the business and delivering work that will help them solve their challenges.

The greatest compliment we can be paid is when a client says, "You understand it! It's like you guys know our business!"

During a conversation, people appreciate someone who can comprehensively get to the point that everyone else has been skirting. After all, if you can understand what the true nature of the problem is, you're going to be more likely to solve it.

That ability to see through to the essence of something will also help you to learn. It helps you to explain something to yourself, and to keep that lesson with you. It certainly stood me in good stead when I was a young intern making my way. You're in a new environment, you're being bombarded with a thousand new experiences ... You need to be able to understand what's going on, and apply that understanding quickly, almost instantly.

There are levels to this thing. The text and the subtext. What people are saying, and what they are doing. What they're saying, and what they're *not* saying. What they say, and what they mean. Often this is completely innocent. At other times, there might be ulterior motives. As a communications worker, you need to be able to pick up these subtle nuances, interpret them and then still deliver the work. After a few years in the industry, you develop a kind of intuition. You might be in a room with a large group of people for the first time. You need to communicate a message, but who is the best person to address it to? Who is the most important person? Who do you need to convince? Sometimes it's the highest-ranking officer of the organisation. The one making the final decision. But sometimes they have a colleague whose opinion they trust implicitly. If you can get that person on your side, they will help you win over the CEO, or the managing director.

Someone must be accountable for the big decisions – usually that's the boss. But sometimes it will be the deputy or the strategist or the divisional manager who really *makes* the decisions. In the communications business – and we're all in the communications business – you need to be aware of all of this. You need to be able to read a room, read what's not being said in a two-line email. Distinguish between what someone says, and what they really want.

In South Africa especially, we don't always enjoy conflict. Often, if we can avoid a negative comment, we will. We will use euphemisms, or even say the exact opposite of what we mean. Just consider this conversation:

"So ... I got your quote ..."

"Okay. And what did you think?"

"It's fine. Ja, no. It's fine."

"We can always negotiate a better rate if you prefer ..."

"No, no. Don't worry."

Clearly, in this situation, the client is *really* not happy with the quote, even though they're saying exactly the opposite. In the client's mind, the quote is hopelessly too high, and they're already five to choosing another supplier. This current supplier is sensing it, and trying to keep the door open for further negotiation, but it looks like it's too late already.

This is a fairly common situation in business. Not everyone's rates will be to the liking of their potential client's. It's up to the client to decide how badly they want to work with the supplier and for the supplier to determine how badly they need the work. From there, negotiations can proceed. Ideally, cost negotiations should be handled by experts, as it's a highly specialised field. But again, it requires sophisticated levels of communication. I believe in winning the client over with my ideas, and then leaving the invoices to take care of themselves – once we are psychologically bound to each other, fellow believers in an idea that can really make a difference.

That is what success looks like, but we also need to accept we won't always succeed, and that not every cost estimate will be to a client's liking. Not every idea will land. My solution will not always be your solution. I often recall this aphorism: "You need to have a good relationship with failure". Life will work out in its own way, at its own pace. There will be successes and setbacks. All are part of the fascinating, rich tapestry of existence.

20

Let's unite for success

I AM GRATEFUL FOR the chance to tell some of my stories, but I remind myself daily that my success is down to other people. I am blessed to be surrounded by an amazing group that elevates me and helps me bring the greatest ideas to fruition. In my business, there is so much real love between my team and me. I really cannot express how much I appreciate that.

I am surrounded by a team of black talent that is making waves in a previously white-dominated industry. The naysayers said it would be impossible to thrive as a black agency – but we are here doing our thing. In 2018, we won Best Mid-sized Public Relations Consultancy at our industry's prestigious Prism awards. In 2019, we won the Campaign of the Year award. We've been killing it!

I was recently blessed to be married to my partner in an incredible ceremony in Cape Town. We put on a magical event at the Zeitz Museum of Contemporary Art Africa. It is a unique venue, a space with no equal that I have seen, and the only place that we felt could do justice to such a ceremony. We got to make our partnership official, and our small group of family and friends got to celebrate with us. I had the night of my life, but anyone who's been married will also know what a relief it can be to finally have the formalities over and done with.

But it wasn't over yet! I got back to work, and the team had put together this elaborate, incredible surprise to congratulate us. I had just come back from declaring my love to my partner, only to walk into another deep, sincere affirmation of love from my team. It was such a powerful moment. It really brought home to me the power of love, and the power of having that love expressed. When we know we are loved, we really are capable of anything!

Of course, life won't always be plain sailing. Love can help us succeed, but it can also help us overcome. I pray constantly for the strength to overcome. I am very aware of the fact that while I may have had some success in my career and in my business, there have also been some setbacks. I expect the road ahead will be similar. There will be stones in my pathway, and I will need help to get past them. I have prayed for that help, that strength, that ability as an entrepreneur. Nothing is guaranteed. We need to be grateful for what we have been able to achieve, and to pray for the strength to achieve more in the future. We will have to make tough choices, and we will also need the wisdom to know the right options to choose.

As I write this, I've come through an intense period of my life. In the past year, I've got engaged, and got married, but I've also just come through one of the toughest years imaginable from a business point of view.

Many, many other business people I've spoken to have expressed the same feelings. Doing business in Africa, in a sluggish economy, is not easy. As much as we remain optimistic, share advice and insights, try to motivate each other, a large part of the business environment we operate in is externally determined. We have our economic context imposed upon us. While it is up to us to make the most of it, there are limits to what we can achieve from our position in the economy. This is precisely the reason we need to become involved in civil society. A wack economy doesn't just happen of its own accord – it is the result of poor management and stewardship. Getting involved in the running of the country, or our governing parties, is a way to start making a difference. The corollary to this is that if you don't get involved in the civic matters, you will have a society imposed on you that you are powerless to influence.

It's crucial to join a community, for the support that it offers in a spiritual, psychological and material sense. But community engagement comes with responsibilities. In the townships, we understand this, because community solidarity is what helped us survive and even overcome the state of oppression that was part of our lives for so long. Each community has its own culture and manner of looking after its interests. This speaks to culture and, when we join a new community, it often requires a period of acclimatising before we can join in and start representing with everybody else.

This was my situation when I arrived at university. Fascinating place, I thought, but how do they share a community? A university is interesting, because it's something of a synthetic society. People have come from across the country and the continent to study in a wide range of fields. They are generally young, but their families are from various cultures and income groups. They are thrust together into a new situation, with their studies and the shared student experience as their greatest common interest. Around that, they build their community. Similar things happen in workplaces, where we find ourselves thrown together by our employers, and then build a workers' community around our shared interests as employees.

This doesn't happen automatically. While humans have an affinity for banding together, modern city living also tends to alienate us from each other. We are so much stronger together, though! We need to resist the impulse towards suffering in solitary isolation. Divided, we are sitting ducks for exploitation. Together, we can have real power – economic power, psychological power, and the power to effect social change. Everyone knows this, especially those forces that would exploit us. History is thus a story of groups banding together while breaking other groups apart. Uniting to defend their own interests, while trying to prevent rival groups from doing the same.

Business is like this. The more communities we build, the greater the success we will achieve. Every community we form gives us more power. Our networks are our power. In business, this could mean joining a union, or an industry association. It might mean joining an international users' community online. It might mean joining a civil initiative against corruption or seeking to achieve some kind of social change. It might just mean making friends at work and discussing your shared workplace issues. Every time you try to join such a group, there will be obstacles. Obstacles of time, expense, inconvenience. You would have work commitments, so you will battle to attend a meeting. You'll struggle to make friends in the office because you're just so ridiculously busy … There might even be policies that actively discourage labour organising in your industry. So much is being done to divide us.

Your success will reflect on yourself as a person, but it will not be all yours. You will succeed according to your ability to get other people to support your ideas. You will see the future, and touch the sky by standing on the shoulders of others.

It's impossible to succeed alone. Even the greatest solo artists of our times – Madonna, for instance – can only be a success because there are several million people who relate to what she does. And while Madge might only have *her* name on the cover art of her incredible music and video releases, they are born of the most extensive creative and business network imaginable. Madonna is one artist, but Madonna is a collective. Madonna is a business. Beyoncé is a business!

We need to look at ourselves in a similar way, as black business people. We are individuals, but our success is predicated upon our ability to build networks. I have tried to continually build such networks in my career. One enemy is one too many. Every contact we make should be a potential partner, supplier, client, mentor or mentee. Let us unite for success. And let us resist those who try to turn us into desperate, self-centred individuals. Ignore and actively oppose those who want to divide us into rival groups according to race, income, culture, language or social category. Don't let them make us hate each other!

To get ahead in brand communication – and in business – you've got to engage, you've got to integrate. At the same time, our society is plagued with much resentment. Much of that resentment is pointless; some of it has been stirred up by interest groups that hope to benefit from polarising us; and some resentment is justified. But even that justified resentment, perhaps based on years of exploitation or past injustices, needs to be overcome. Even a perfectly valid grievance can be like poison, if we carry it around with us, nursing it like our entire reason for being. Like a survivor bent on vengeance. If we have grievances, we need to air them and address them and secure reparations, so that the wound can heal. We need to have the difficult conversations – between individuals, between groups and within groups.

Two of the driving determinants of success are ability and opportunity. The one usually leads to the other. If someone has ability, they will find opportunities. Once we find opportunities, we build up experience and grow our ability. Our racist past under apartheid was about depriving black people of opportunities and the chance to grow their ability. Today, under our more democratic dispensation, we are trying to correct the wrongs of the past by making sure people get the opportunities they deserve.

The process of building a democratic state has not been plain sailing. The governments we have formed have been imperfect – if not fundamentally corrupt – with much room for improvement. Society, and business as part of that society, have a responsibility to try to help the government correct itself. There are many ways to do this.

When I was at Nando's, we managed to strike a good balance between socially aware political messaging, marketing and entertainment. It got us into a fair amount of trouble too – but that's how you know you're doing it right. One of our most notorious – and successful – campaigns was for something we called the "Idlanathi Meal". There were four different ads in this campaign, which poked fun at government fat cats who were "cutting back" on their extravagant spending, but still living hopelessly lavish lifestyles.

"As MPs, we've been lambasted for overspending," said a character in one advert, as he climbed into a golf cart on a lush golf course. "So, in the interest of ordinary South Africans, I got me a more modest car."

We then panned across to his ride, a shiny black convertible.

"As a minister, I have to be more careful about my overspending," said another fat cat MP, reclining in her swimsuit with a cocktail on the stairs of her swimming pool. "So, I've moved to a more humble home."

We pulled wide to reveal her multi-storey new crib, complete with bodyguards and the house help pruning her topiary.

The pay-off was the Nando's man telling us how we had also learned to tighten our belts in these tough economic times, which is why we are offering this Nando's quarter chicken and chips deal.

The big idea: "Now, *that's* responsible spending!"

This was the kind of topical commentary that became a feature of Nando's campaigns. Showing that we were politically engaged, but with the sense of humour to make fun of the political situation, and to use it as a hook to market our delicious chicken offerings.

When we first came out with that approach, hardly any other brands were being this outspoken. Topical political commentary in the marketing space was hardly a thing. Despite our history of award-winning creative work, the South African advertising industry had actually been rather conservative. The Nando's approach was about changing a culture, as much as using an edgy tone.

There is a generational component to this too: the way things have always been done, compared to the way the new breed would like to do things. There will always be friction when that happens, and it will depend on the individuals in the various roles whether that friction will just be incidental, or lead to the death of progress.

Generational shifts are happening in our country's political environment, across numerous business sectors and indeed in the ethical principles of our people at large. There is the old way of thinking, and then there is the new way. It will manifest in different forms in every industry, but there will be struggles fought in every such arena around how the generational shift will occur. Sometimes, change happens gradually and peacefully. Other times, it is violent and revolutionary. Sometimes it needs a movement, complete with manifestoes and written sets of values. As an individual, you are also likely to find yourself swept along in these periods of change, and you will have to choose sides. Doing that will be easier, the more settled you are with your own personal values. I believe that the more principled we are, the easier it is to make a principled stand.

But organisational culture is powerful, and a newcomer can find it difficult to resist. You might come in and become swallowed up in a set of exploitive, bigoted values. We may be won over by the promise of material benefits. We get corrupted ...

As leaders of organisations, I think we need to constantly be aware of this. We need to think about the culture of our enterprises, what values that reflects. What is the deeper purpose of the business we're running? That purpose is crucial, because our organisational culture evolves in service of that purpose. Is our purpose sincere? Do we say one thing on our website, and do something quite different when we deal with our customers and when we manage our people?

Managers and executives need to keep asking themselves these kinds of questions – I know I do. Culture is strange. It can change and shift from something positive to something quite harmful if it is not constantly monitored and consciously managed. It's a little simplistic to think that the odd young, idealistic hire will help to keep your organisation's culture fresh and dynamic. A newbie will find it easier to fit in than to try to change a place. That is how culture abides, and legacy, reactionary values survive within an organisation. I have heard it said that the best way to really change an enterprise is through mass hiring, which can make a big difference in a short period of time. For instance, move your organisation towards greater gender representation by hiring women in packs. Hire four women, instead of just one woman, who might find herself overwhelmed and marginalised in a male-dominated environment. Transform your business by employing a cohort of five new professionals, all black, and see what that does to the culture of the firm!

Change needs a movement. A transition requires a critical mass to gain momentum. I'm confident that ours is a generation that will drive that kind of change. There is some magic in the air. There are going to be many transitions.

21

A terrain of digital struggle

I BELIEVE IN OUR country – in what we have achieved, and in what we are still capable of achieving. There are social changes required, and political ones. A lot of change will take place in the technological arena, and many changes will happen because of our new media environment. Of course, these areas are not unrelated. Many countries have seen massive social change that was facilitated by social media and other digital platforms. That change hasn't always been positive.

Donald Trump's rise to power happened on the back of personality profiling and targeted social-media advertising. Brexit was driven as much by a marketing campaign as by any fundamental, factual messaging. The Arab Spring was a popular uprising driven by social media, but its outcomes have been mixed. In South Africa, PR campaigns by Bell Pottinger and their henchmen used social media to polarise our nation and create deep racial divisions that we are still working to heal. Digital media is a tool, a platform, but also a terrain of struggle, which can be used in service of good or evil.

As communications workers, we need to understand how to use it and how to protect against its misuse. The new media can be used to manipulate and to do harm. Algorithms and bots are launched to drive particular agendas. Our behaviour is being shaped by the media we consume, and we're not always aware that it's happening. A social media platform like Facebook gives us such a curated view of the world, tailored to confirm what the tech company has decided are our views. We thus become trapped in an echo chamber with a handful of like-minded people, confirming each other's biases, all of which have also been created and fed by algorithms.

If our most basic political opinions and value systems can be manipulated through social media, imagine how effectively our brand choices can be influenced! This is the media space that modern marketing operates in. It's powerful, it's a bit scary, but it's not going anywhere. Communications professionals need to be intimately familiar with social media, and consumers need to maintain a healthy critical scepticism about the messages they are exposed to. There's a funny little ethical boundary somewhere inside all of this, and it's sometimes hard to read.

Media is a brutal space these days. We may have much of our news and social-contact experience curated for us, but certain content is unavoidable. To work in media today, we need a bit of a thick skin. You need to be the type of person who can handle it. Natural disasters – the utter devastation of a flood, an earthquake, a tsunami – they are brought into our lives as they happen, allowing us to raise awareness and rally assistance, but also shocking us with the sheer humanity of these events. Terrorist events now also have an almost insufferably evil social media element, amplifying the impact of these shocking acts right across the planet. Any acts of violence can also be captured on the video-enabled smartphones we all now carry, raising awareness, but also simply spreading the disease, infecting more of us with the values of violence.

It's terrifying, but also an amazing example of the complexity of human beings that we have such violent depravity inside us, alongside the magical empathy that enables us to help each other through the greatest hardships. We can count ourselves blessed that while we create such difficulties for ourselves, our neighbours and our planet, we also have the ability to resolve them.

22

Home is where the heart is

INSIDE THIS WHIRLWIND of complexity, I am committed to making things work – in my relationships, in my business, in my country and in my world. As far as my home country goes, I feel committed to building South Africa – one hundred per cent at all times, in all ways. I was born and bred here. I would be able to move overseas, to live anywhere in the English-speaking world, with my skill. But philosophically, I've not been able to make peace with that idea.

It's quite miraculous what we've achieved. Despite the trouble we find ourselves in at the moment – directionless leadership, an energy crisis, massive unemployment, a stagnant economy – I remain defiantly optimistic. I believe we need leaders who can dream big to lift us as a country. It takes vision, as well as leadership, to turn that vision into reality. With my marriage, my family and my business, I have thrown in my lot with this country, and I am committed to making a go of things here in South Africa. I'm constantly looking for a vision that I can relate to, so that I can commit my energies to working for it.

All around the world, there are examples of countries that have lifted themselves up from almost nothing. Singapore. Hong Kong. Those places were tiny backwaters with almost no natural resources. Now they are global financial capitals. South Africa has so much more to start with. We too can be great!

When I visited Hong Kong, I felt like I was reminded of the possible future. We stayed in a hotel downtown, and when it was time to leave, the concierge asked us, "Check out straight to the airport, gentlemen?"

"What do you mean?" I asked.

Then I realised that several airlines had check-in counters operating within the hotel. Emirates, British Airways, Swissair, Lufthansa … you name it. The downstairs lobby looked like you'd expect an airport check-in hall to look. I was able to check in my luggage from inside the hotel, and then head out into Hong Kong with a day pack for a last couple of hours' sightseeing. That is innovative thinking right there. To think that travellers have been lugging their bags around with them for decades when all we really want to do is send them off ahead of us. Check-in counters inside the hotels! I guess you can tell I was pretty impressed.

And that can be us! Every single time I come back to Joburg, I dream of my country being like that. With world-class public transport integrated into the business and hospitality infrastructure, so I can be where I need to be, almost as soon as I get the idea! A Gautrain network that comes to my office, and connects me to Durban. An integrated mobility solution that links minibus taxis, BRT buses, light rail and private vehicles seamlessly. We must be able to design and build such a system – and when we do, the country is going to expand exponentially!

It was South African visionaries who drew up our National Development Plan (NDP) about a decade ago. Not just visionaries, but visionaries with a plan! That plan reads like poetry in places; it offers an artistic and practical vision for addressing our country's triple challenges of poverty, unemployment and inequality. Whether from a lack of political will, institutional politics or the rise of materialism in our government, we have not been able to implement the NDP as well as we should have. We are having a different set of conversations today compared to 2013, when the NDP 2030 was first published.

I love the passion that went into that NDP planning, and it breaks my heart that such vision and passion could not be realised. It was an opportunity missed. Perhaps it can yet be revived and brought to fruition. A plan in the hands of people committed to uplifting our country may experience far more success. Even if there might have been a shortage of commitment in some quarters of our implementing agencies, there are thousands, millions of South Africans who *do* have that commitment. People care about this country. We need to spread that sense of caring, and work together to uplift each other, because the alternatives are diabolical.

I have seen the alternative to working together for a common interest: selfishness. As a business owner, I know that temptation only too well, the temptation to just turn inwards and look after your own interests. As entrepreneurs – black entrepreneurs – our business receives no government assistance whatsoever, no subsidies, grants or development funding. I may get some SETA training funding – R3 000 here or there. When I hear about government funds being misused, or budgets allocated and not spent, I can't help speculating what we might be able to do with that amount of money in our business.

When I hear about R38 million being spent on a website, I think about what R38 million would buy you in a business like ours – a bona fide, 100 per cent black-owned marketing business. I think I could probably have employed three times the number of people that we have today. If we're worried about unemployment, and young people who aren't being trained, a good place to start is by doing some due diligence on legitimate black businesses and supporting us. We do exist! We're out here doing the things!

With development grants, we would be able to finance university studies for our existing staff, we could employ more people. As a small business owner, I'm diligent in following the law. But our government has not been too willing to support a business like ours. We are a 100 per cent black-owned, 100 per cent black-staffed, legitimate, capable, working business. I'm wondering what kind of businesses they *are* supporting. While I am curious about what kind of enterprises the government chooses to do business with, we don't need their support. Our success is not dependent on state patronage. We are part of the private sector, and our business network is primarily located there.

It's easy to become cynical and jaded about state patronage networks. I sometimes feel that if the government wanted to do something about practically supporting small businesses, they would have done something a long time ago. It wouldn't have involved any extra expense – they would simply have had to ensure that their existing suppliers were paid on time. It's the death knell to a small business for a significant invoice to go unpaid for months.

Instead, some public institutions are mismanaged to the point where they have to send out communiques to the industry at large, saying, "Sorry, we're not going to be able to pay you. We'll pay you when we can afford to."

Our business is on those mailing lists too, but fortunately we have hardly any government business. My heart bleeds for those companies that are dependent on that work to keep going, to pay their staff salaries and to pay their own suppliers! When the SABC can't pay suppliers, productions grind to a halt and the effects trickle down to the entire TV production and media industry.

On the other hand, one can appreciate the government's position, as it needs to allocate fiscal budgets so it can keep our country's electricity supply running. It has struggled to do this, which shows a further lack of true determination to do right by our people. If the government really wants to do something, it will do it. The failure to deliver services to our people simply demonstrates that we are not their priority. Other interests have been placed ahead of the people. What those interests are, we can only speculate: patronage, self-enrichment, crony capitalism?

When state resources are seen as a cash cow, instead of a powerful tool to uplift our people, we have lost our way. Commissions of inquiry into state corruption have revealed a vast network of maladministration. This is itself a good thing, as it indicates some willingness to change course and to follow an ethical path of using the state to uplift our people. But what the inquiries reveal is disturbing in the extreme. These revelations will continue. There are links between the instances of wrongdoing, and one expects that one revelation will lead to another. It's all connected. The full truth will emerge one day. Everyone's garbage must eventually come out for collection. The system of looting has been in place for several years, and many people are complicit.

Instead of trying to concoct complex methods of reallocating funds and then covering up their tracks to escape prosecution, our gifted civil servants should apply creativity to what they are meant to do. Why not just get the fundamentals in place? Why not use the state apparatus to deliver for the people of South Africa?

It can sometimes seem that customer service only survives in the private sector, where we are dependent on creating positive client experiences and building relationships. We give great service because it leads to great business. The public sector, often blessed with a captive market, can slip into a situation of disrespecting the public it is meant to serve, because the public have no other options.

"They are going to have to come back to us anyway," becomes the attitude. "So why should we bother giving them the service we are supposed to provide?"

23

A foot in the door

BACK DURING MY university days, I walked into FCB and hustled myself a position as an intern – one of only 12 selected for the Iziko internship programme. The advertising industry back then was definitely a rock-n-roll type of environment. The style of the office décor was like nothing I had ever seen before, and the vibe was positive, dynamic and creative.

For a young person dreaming of a career in advertising, cracking an internship at FCB was like reaching nirvana. It was incredible. The offices, at the bottom of Fredman Drive in Sandton, had a great bar, with games and all sorts of entertainment. There were cunning ways of stimulating ideas as well as blowing off steam. That agency, around the turn of the millennium, had managed to strike the perfect balance between work and play. It provided me with an incredible foundation. It was the genesis of my career, my entry into the real world of the creative economy. I had worked before, but this was a career, a profession. When I got in there, I *knew* I was in advertising.

FCB had big clients, serious accounts. Cell phone service provider Vodacom had chosen FCB to handle their brand business. Toyota, Tiger Brands ... Many of the big guys were there and, in a lot of ways, FCB was the top agency in the country at the time. There were about 500 of the most talented people in the industry in that building, so it was the ideal place to be for a kid looking to learn and to be inspired.

FCB set an interesting tone, which I have taken with me over the subsequent years. The agency has produced some incredible thinkers during its history, but I was really blessed to be there at a particularly special time. I know it's a common conceit to say, "I was there during the glory days," but, in my case, I really feel that I was. Those of us who were there at that time forged bonds and relationships that have stayed with us ever since. That time at FCB was when I started setting up my industry network, which has served me with excellence and aplomb ever since. I laugh about it today, implying that it was some kind of "nursery of success", but the 12 of us in that intake of interns have gone on to do rather well in the industry.

That applies to all of us, across every industry. The friends and acquaintances we make when we're starting out will serve us throughout our career. Some will fade out of our lives, but others will rise to become significant players in our sector. Perhaps we ourselves will become big players, with something to offer our friends, partnerships to build, arrangements to make, simple loyalties to live up to. Passing on each other's contact details, or emailing a query to an old friend. Perhaps we'll only catch up once or twice a year, maybe over a FaceTime chat, but those relationships are crucial. We must nurture and value our friendships, for they are precious. When we first get to know each other, we might be fellow interns, still at university, taking taxis to work. But that doesn't make our friendship any less valuable. Properly nurtured, that relationship can grow and deepen, with us sharing advice and experiences as we work our way up the corporate ladder. You'd be surprised how quickly time flies. Pretty soon, the two of you will be senior executives, with some serious decisions to make, and some deep industry experience. If you've kept your friendship healthy, you'll be able to provide each other with invaluable support and advice, and to share access to the rest of your respective networks.

In my case, many of us who started out together have gone on to achieve successes, thanks to the foundation laid at that agency. We were looked after, mentored and trained. There was a huge focus on training. Many of us from that generation have taken what we learned and infused it into our own businesses, into the way things are done at our agencies. It was an incredible foundation, which we have each built upon with our learnings from the other agencies and companies we moved on to later in our careers. In this way, we each collect knowledge and experience, curating it, choosing which pieces are most relevant to us and our journey, and then putting it all together to create our own unique methods.

Then we go on to start businesses of our own, where we induct and mentor a new generation of young professionals, and the process begins again. For me, I kept learning throughout my time at FCB, which equipped me to be an even more efficient and open-minded learner in my subsequent time at Ogilvy, DDB, at Nando's and at MTV.

Lessons can come from anywhere. The eccentric copy editor can have industry insights to share that are every bit as valuable as the sage advice from the company CEO or the managing director. I try not to judge advice according to its provenance, but according to its value to me and my life. The key to unlocking this knowledge is to relate to everyone you meet in an open, sincere and respectful way that encourages them to share their experience with you. Sharing advice is one of the greatest acts of generosity, because there is seldom anything in it for us. It's all about enriching someone else's life, from the well of our own experience, and out of the goodness of our hearts. The only criterion is usually whether we think the person we're advising will take our tips on board. Will they take them seriously and consider applying them? Essentially, it's about respect. Everyone can learn something from the next person, so it is important to be curious, and interested in what other people do, or how they understand their industry. You'll be fascinated by what they have to share.

Soon enough, you will have filled a treasure trove of wisdom in your mind. There will be hundreds of little proverbs or anecdotes in there. Little shortcuts that make work quicker, or techniques that help you see through the haze of stress and hustle and identify the reality of a situation. I'm not always able to remember exactly where I acquired a particular piece of wisdom, but, if it's useful, you can bet I'll hang onto it, keep it with the rest of my pearls!

I've been lucky to work with some incredibly humble bosses. There were many moments where I sat with the CEO as an intern, after I'd rather bravely come into his office and asked, "What are you doing?"

I also have a physical treasure trove at home: an old box where I keep mementos from my career. Going through it recently, I found letters from my earliest bosses, often with a single sentence of priceless advice, in their own handwriting. I take it as an enormous compliment that they saw fit to write me those letters and to impart such heartfelt advice. My clumsy mix of brash bravado and humility seems to have worked for me.

————•————

After a few months as a junior account executive at FCB, I was promoted to account executive in the client services division. It sometimes came with a kind email of introduction – cc'd to me – to the clients I would be working with: "Please meet Sylvester. We've been highly impressed with his work, and he has been promoted to account executive. We're proud to have him on your account, and we have complete confidence that the two of you will work well together."

Those letters would boost me into my new role. It's such an encouragement to know that your seniors are proud of your ability. I had a sense of being elevated and pushed because I was in a space where people wanted me to succeed – for my own good, as well as the good of the company. They wanted me to do well. These were the early days of real transformation. Our internship programme had been set up with the sincere goal of growing industry leaders for the future. Looking at the careers of my fellow interns, I see that it did exactly that. Initiator and industry great Nkwenkwe Nkomo must be proud – I owe him everything!

————•————

Whatever industry you find yourself in, it might be useful to consider this approach. Some people call it "doing an industry job" – doing something that will benefit your entire sector, not just your company. Indeed, often a person we have trained will leave our company soon after their training has begun bearing fruit. At such a time, it's tempting to feel let down or betrayed. You've invested weeks, months or years in developing this person, and now some other company is going to reap the benefits of that training. But that's a simplistic view. We educate and train our colleagues for the benefit of our entire industry, and broader society, so that they can deliver a better service. It's not just about them being productive employees for our company. Training is really a privilege for the trainer. It is an opportunity for them to enrich the world by passing down their learnings to the next generation. It's the same reason we bring up children. We don't do it simply so that they will be able to look after us when we're old. We bring up our children to the best of our ability because they are our gift to the world. The world will gain most of the benefit – not us.

I grab every opportunity I get to train my colleagues – whether it is through formal training programmes or just a friendly comment or two while we're working on an assignment together. Those opportunities are invaluable to me, as they give me purpose. By passing along some wisdom I have picked up – probably from someone else who mentored me when I was young – I am giving my little role here at the company some purpose. I give my life meaning. I also really believe in the importance of my industry. Communications is a vital part of the fabric of modern life. If I can improve the way our industry delivers its service, I consider that a privilege. I will be but a link in the long chain of my industry's development, stretching back decades, *centuries*, to the dawn of human communication. One hopes we're gradually getting better at communicating and I'm proud to play my small role. The entire point of communication is to share knowledge, after all, so it would be strange for a communications person to be reluctant to share what insights they have. We must be the poster boys for knowledge sharing – in the interests of our organisation, our community and the human race!

You start to notice this with the people who become industry leaders. They work for the good of their company, but they have another broader perspective, looking out for the interests of everyone.

There is knowledge, but there is also magic. We can teach knowledge, but we cannot teach magic. That must come at its own time. We can describe ways that encourage magic, methods of working – brainstorms, blue-sky meditations, pitches, motivations, synopses, outlines and manifestos – but we cannot summon the magic at will. The dope idea that leads the campaign, tying everything together and making it awesome, that idea will come from the sky, it will pop into someone's head almost randomly. It is a little understood area, this magic, but it must be taken very seriously.

We must open ourselves up to magic. An idea will not always come when we try to force it – anyone who has sat through a fruitless late-afternoon brainstorm will know what I mean. Sometimes the magic idea will pop into our head when we least expect it: while we're driving, watching a series, or on the loo. At other times, an idea that someone else expresses will trigger another idea inside us, and the magic will be a kind of hybrid solution. Like a mash-up; it's an unlikely combination, but it just might work. We must be open to the magic. So many ideas might also seem silly at first, but we must also not dismiss them right away. Organisations thrive on ideas, so they should try to build a culture of taking all suggestions seriously, even the apparently silly ones. By the time a "silly" idea has been developed and added to by the other members of the team, it might be perfectly workable.

The legends of the game that I have been fortunate to work with have certainly had this kind of attitude. That approach helped them create magic. Every creative contribution was welcomed, every suggestion entertained, and developed, discussed, analysed, reverse-engineered and given the full treatment, before we ever decided whether it would or would not work. It was about magic. It was about delivery, flare, making the client look good, doing the things required to be excellent, to be the best we could be, for the benefit of our partners. This approach worked, and the result was some incredible work. The work won us awards across the industry and helped our clients achieve their objectives – sales, brand awareness, calls to action, whatever they were aiming for. We would celebrate that work as well, throwing parties and celebrations in the office. That would get morale up to insane heights, and in turn stimulate more of those incredible ideas that fuel the greatest work.

Oh, the parties! Whether we had an award to celebrate, some props from a client, or we just needed to blow off steam, the Friday after-work sessions in the office bar were legendary. In addition to those parties, once a month, the entire agency would get together to present the best work from the various divisions, to celebrate, but also to learn from it, checking what we had done well, that we might possibly summon the magic back into our minds when our clients once again called upon us to do so. We were acknowledging our achievements, but also constantly pushing ourselves and driving the company forward.

It was such an incredible, incredible foundation! To this day, I find myself posting throwback pics from those days, which proves how relevant my time at that agency still is to my current situation.

PART TWO

24

A first attempt

GOING THROUGH MY box of memories, I came across one of my earliest formal creative endeavours. My first attempt. It was a print advert that I created with pencils, kokis and paper. I must have been 12 or 13 years old when I put it together. I had no training at the time. I knew nothing about composition and visual dynamics. But there it was – an ad, complete with headline, pack shot, body copy and a catchy pay-off line that stuck in your mind. The design wasn't too bad either.

When I look at some of my precocious early efforts like that, I can't help being a little impressed with myself. Not bad for someone who was still at school! I think that school project was an advert for Liqui-Fruit fruit juice. There are signs that I had raw talent – and certainly an interest in advertising – from an early age. But I still required opportunities to convert that potential into effective delivery as a professional. My days at FCB did that.

25

The bidding war

THE INTERNSHIP I BAGGED for myself at that brave, magical agency is what took me into the big time.

I found myself surrounded by incredible women at that agency. Julia Meltzer is the vanguard. Lindi Magida, Mirella Di Pietro, Nicci Kurland, Romaine McKenzie ... these incredible women saw something in me, and really pushed me. They wanted me to do well and they mentored me to ensure that I excelled. They did it in such a relaxed, informal style, but it turned me into a good client-service person. A facilitator in the field of creative execution.

The beauty of the FCB internship programme was that you could rotate across the entire business for a month at a time. I spent a month in the creative department, a month at strategy and a month in client services. I fell in love with the industry all over again! At the end of my rotation, the various department heads got together to decide which of us interns would be deployed to which departments. From what I've heard, the head of strategy said he definitely wanted me in his department.

Client services were similarly interested in me. The decision was made to ask me where I would prefer to start my career. This was encouraging, and a tremendous feather in my cap, but then the question became, which department to choose. I went to speak to the head of the agency and sought his counsel. That's when I realised I was the subject of a bidding war between the departments. "You've shown great strategic ability," he told me. "You'd be a very good strategist. But if you applied that vision to client service, you'd be an even better marketing professional."

He recommended that I learn what I could from strategy, but then use it in a client-service context. That's what I chose to do, and it was the best decision I've ever made. I love people. I love interacting with them. And that is the basis of client service – working with people! I have also never lost my service impulse. I get real satisfaction from serving clients.

There is an art to serving. We teach that art in our company. We've integrated it into our culture. I have no problem sitting in the office writing up strategies, but my work is that much more rewarding when I can get out, meet the client and explain the strategy to them in person. The flexibility of the client service role really works for me. There are many ways that we can help each other.

I do like the honesty of the role being called client service, rather than account management. It's client service, because it's about the personal interaction that underpins our business relationship. As one moves through the industry and you become an entrepreneur, starting your own business, these same principles drive you. Human relationships are the basis of all business. Internal relationships within your company, and relationships with clients. The industry being the way it is, those relationships can also change. Someone who was once your colleague might be your client a few years later. A competitor from a rival agency might later be a partner on another project. These can be monumental relationships, lasting 20 or 25 years, like my friendships with Nunu Ntshingila, Karabo Denalane and Mirella Di Pietro among others.

Julia Meltzer was another. I remember being in the very early stages of my career at FCB, still an intern taking minibus taxis to work. At one point, I needed to travel across town rather urgently. And Julia, a senior exec, who really had no obligation to do me any favours, she just handed me the keys to her Suzuki Vitara SUV and said, "Here, take my car."

That level of trust has nothing to do with the business. That is just pure human kindness and love. She trusted me with her own personal asset. A young guy who had only got his driver's licence a year or two earlier. That's a real vote of confidence. It was incredible. Those are the kind of people I have got to meet and work with during my career. I have been blessed.

Those friendships are unshakeable and they will never be erased. It has set a tone for me. Today, when I think of the classic advertising agency environment, I think of FCB. I also sense that my mentors are watching me at the communications agency I've built, and they're wishing me well – financially, physically and emotionally. If I go back to that agency where I once worked, what is the first thing I see? I walk into the building and I'll meet Lucia, who's been the receptionist since I was a bright-eyed prospect at the same agency. Her greeting will be every bit as warm and comforting as it was back in those days. That's the beauty of this industry.

The marble lobby of the ground floor leads through to the lifts. Then it's through the glass doors and onto the floor of the agency. When you walk in, you know that you're in a creative space. It's colourful, it's beautiful and it's lush. The boardrooms, where so many of those magical ideas are crafted, run down the side of the office. Outside one of them, a line of models is in for a casting. Here a photographer is back from a shoot to share his images. Beautiful chairs and couches adorn the office ... It's just a stylish space. Classy, mind-blowing pieces of artwork on the floor and on the walls. The furniture choices. It's incredible. Entering that agency space was like being in a dream. It generates energy. You cannot help but be inspired. That energy, that creativity, enters you – almost through osmosis. In a space like that, you just become your best self.

I often say that my time in the industry has taught me the power of spatial dynamics. A creative space stimulates creativity. I've done my utmost to create such a space at DNA. I think I've managed to inject some of my aesthetic into the look and feel of our environment. Ours is a warm space – lush, flokati rugs welcome visitors onto the floor, wood textures are everywhere, and oversized framed artworks lean against the walls. The orange glow of vintage filament bulbs lends a gently organic ambience.

We try to balance our clean, digital feel with a classic, analogue sensibility. Our space defines us, but it also energises us. It is our home. Welcoming, encouraging and also inspiring. Even when we're away from the office, it is there in our subconscious. In our personal lives as individuals, knowing that we have a cosy home to go back to is deeply reassuring. It enables us to go out into the world with courage and confidence. The DNA office is all that. It powers us out into the world, and we come back to recharge.

It's not all models and interior design, though. There is also stress, swearing and laughing out loud. Creative tension is sometimes disruptive. But that is like fuel for me. Once I made it onto the permanent staff roster, I would arrive at work early and leave late every single day. "I'm here now", my conduct said. I rose through the ranks, eventually becoming an account manager. I was at that agency for four years before I felt the urge for new experiences and I moved to Ogilvy, another iconic Johannesburg agency.

26

Greener pastures

FCB WAS MY FIRST agency experience. The agency had shaped me, but I could not help wondering what other agencies might be like. Surely there were other ways to do the agency thing? I decided I needed a completely different sort of experience in order to expand my industry awareness. I left FCB as an account manager, and I moved to Ogilvy to become an account director. Getting to shift up the agency totem pole was another incentive to move agencies, but the main reason was certainly to broaden my horizons.

Anyone who has started in a junior position at a company will also know the phenomenon in which you are always seen as the same junior person you were when you arrived. It's not meant to be disrespectful, but sometimes that is just human nature. We develop a way of relating to a person, and we don't change it, even while the person in question grows into a mature, experienced professional. It's no negative reflection on the people at my first company, but, in their minds, I would always be the sassy intern who had the gall to walk into the office and demand a job. I had been little more than a child when I started and, in many people's minds, I would always be that child. If I was going to change people's perceptions, I needed to go off and do something different. I needed new challenges and wider experiences to validate myself. The FCB environment had helped me grow, and I had grabbed the opportunities with both hands, but for my next phase of growth I needed to move. The Ogilvy opportunity arose, and I knew it was time …

My move to Ogilvy was really about getting to work on new accounts, big accounts that would teach me how other large brands do things. Ogilvy had the Coca-Cola account at the time, and it doesn't get much bigger than that.

Ogilvy is another global agency steeped in history. They were doing some amazing work at the time, with a staff of incredibly courageous creative people, many of whom I still have great relationships with today. The move to Ogilvy was exactly what I needed at the time, for the next stage of my education. I was there for just a year, though. Then I was out of there.

The reason for my short stay at Ogilvy is not that I was unhappy, or I didn't fit in there, but that the pace of my growth had picked up exponentially. Don't get me wrong. I learned a great deal at the new agency. The culture there was totally different to the one I had just left. Ogilvy was about doing the work, well and professionally. I also learned the importance of structured ways of working, and the value of integrating different skills into your client offering. Ogilvy were masters of the "way" of working, who did what, how to broaden solutions using the various capabilities in the business. I found a sure understanding of the way things should work. I learned so much! Personality-wise, though, such a structured way of working doesn't come naturally to me.

I have a looser, more instinctive approach to coming up with ideas. But I learned the value of combining that creative impulse with efficient, effective systems to get the work through the pipeline – from ideas to production to delivery.

Every agency has its own vibe and style of operating, its own energy. Ogilvy's was not really the same as mine, at that stage of my life. That's not necessarily a judgment, it's just a reflection of where I was personally. Ogilvy also didn't feel like an agency on the cutting edge compared to where I had come from. Certainly, I didn't find the physical space as inspiring! Perhaps it was a little more corporate. It felt like work to me.

Looking back, I find this such an interesting time of my life. The move had taught me that I had mastered many of the hard skills of marketing. I could interpret client needs and plot a strategic direction for them. I could map a suite of media services onto that strategy, then zoom in, down to a micro scale, and visualise what creative executions we could provide in service of the strategy. Throughout the process, I could manage the client relationship, have enough cultural awareness to know how the client's brand and its messaging fitted into society, and also adjust to the client's shifting needs within that. I could consult, interpret briefs and provide advice. I had pretty much got the hang of the profession. But now it was time for the next stage of my development – my journey to personal fulfilment and expression of my own vision for how the business of marketing could be handled.

Ogilvy had a culture of "Do the work well, do it efficiently, within deadline and go home". I really appreciated that. It made me realise that creative execution needn't be a rambling, drawn-out process. I also thoroughly enjoyed the clients I got to work with. Again, it gave me the chance to build incredible relationships, with clients who later became colleagues, colleagues who would later be my competitors, and co-workers who would later cross the floor and become CEOs and marketing managers in the corporate world. Many industry connections were built in that year and a bit.

I was still young by the time I got to Ogilvy. The more corporate environment was a bit of a shock to me, and while I did adapt, I still dearly missed the FCB world. To be honest, I pined for those days of crazy, gay abandon in that plush, creative whirlpool. I missed the people who made the place so special. The friends and colleagues I had learned so much from and learned such valuable lessons with. So, what did I do? What any impulsive 23-year-old would do. I went back to FCB!

As fate tends to do, it led me to bump into a former friend and manager from FCB. Chats were had, offers were made, and, before you knew it, I was back where I started. At my former agency.

I immediately realised I had made a terrible mistake.

I had left that same agency wanting to explore other ways of doing things. I had done a bit of that, but nowhere near enough. I had learned all I needed from FCB, and while I loved the environment and the joy of working with my friends again, I had seen this movie before. Besides my excursion to Ogilvy, I hadn't yet explored the map that much. I had not quite returned the conquering hero, so I slotted back into the roles and relationships I had filled previously. There was a bit of a hangover from my previous spell – not even in a bad way, but the same group of people will tend to relate in the same way. I saw that I wasn't going to be growing or evolving in the same environment.

The explorer in me felt let down. I wanted to get out and see more, do more! I needed to keep learning. I had learned the hard skills, but I had so much more to discover about the soft skills, the subtle but deep ways of working that come from a real, visceral understanding of what you're doing. Within a year I would be out of FCB, this time for keeps.

27

Smaller, but bigger

DDB WORLDWIDE COMMUNICATIONS Group. DDB! This would be a smaller operation, with fewer than 15 staff. At the time it was so boutique it was almost a start-up. DDB had been around for a very long time, but it was in the middle of a serious reinvigoration process, and it felt fresh!

By this time, my needs were different. I no longer looked at an agency for what a young person considers important – the facilities. I now looked for growth potential. What could I learn? How could I grow myself to be more useful, more effective, better? I was also ready to be challenged. I knew I was capable of more, and I was ready to stretch my legs as a professional and as a leader. I knew I could add value, and I was hungry for a chance to demonstrate that.

My skills were good, I had developed my own way of managing people. There were no issues with me then, if I say so myself. I could do the work, I could take it to new levels, and I was ready do that, with people and clients who were similarly brave and ambitious. I was not at DDB to slack off. I was there to grab the future!

I had grown up, I needed something more from my work, and I found it at DDB. I had no way of knowing quite what that would be, but DDB was where I fell in love with solving problems.

I had a really cool office to myself, with a meeting room coming off the side of it. I was starting to move up in the world, and my set-up was starting to reflect that. I was in a responsible, senior position, with all its attendant opportunities and stresses, but I had the added bonus of working in a small agency, which allowed me to have input into every aspect of the business. I would lock myself in that office and craft ideas, power out work until it felt like there was steam coming out of my ears!

Wow, what an amazing job! It all started coming together at DDB; I started thinking bigger. I started knowing that I have a strength. I can do this thing. A large part of the economy runs on confidence, and people work the same way. The more confident we become in our own abilities, the greater those abilities become. This creates a self-elevating loop that really fuels the best work. I was able to contribute to shaping the agency's internal strategy in a way that would get bought in a beautiful way. After that point I was churning out successful campaigns, managing the creative output to the client, the alignment to their needs. I was moving with true visionaries, having the most incredible, high-level conversations, debates on strategy for global brands like Unilever and the like. And I was being taken seriously. My ideas were being implemented!

Within a few months of my joining DDB, I had really hit my stride. I couldn't believe the value that was coming out of me. The work we were doing was incredibly impactful. The inspirational people I worked with shaped me even further. DDB's heritage reaches back to one of its founders, Bill Bernbach – a legend of advertising. DDB had appointed an illustrious London ad agency man, Glen Lomas, to run the Johannesburg operation, and working with him was another major education for me. The experience of seeing him at work gave me the understanding to approach brand problems with confidence. I started getting a little of that supreme self-belief that is common to the best strategists, the utter certainty. Of knowing that *this* is the strategy. *This* is what you want to do in this situation!

This was an evolution further away from my earlier client-service orientation, where the relationship is everything, and the client's wishes are paramount. When I was working in client service, I found myself often trying to decode clients' thinking, asking how they saw things, so that I could better give them what they wanted. Now I wasn't too concerned about taking orders. I was writing strategy and setting the agenda, alongside the managing director.

Years on from that internship bidding war at my first agency, where I was torn between joining the strategy division or client service, fate had brought me back to the same fork in the road. Back at the start of my career, I had chosen client services. This time I chose strategy. That was where my brain was now: analysing the approach even more.

I got to work on some really beautiful client strategies. I learned to identify the essential challenge of every account. Was this a brand-building job? Or was the main challenge around their business fundamentals – their sales, their market share? There are strategies that work in each of these situations. They need to be tailored to suit the client and the market. The client also needs to have complete confidence that your analysis is right and that your strategic solution is the right one. That requires concrete research and data analytics. Understanding comes from fact finding, learning what is happening in the market, what attitudes drive brand awareness and understanding how to reach people.

I had a lot to offer by this stage, so I wasn't just running on confidence. DDB built my confidence in solving problems for them because they let me be at the front line, I was allowed – no, *encouraged* – to venture into the big conversations, because they believed that I could provide the right solutions. It was so empowering to have an agency show that much faith in me and my ability. That is how you grow talent – give your staff real decision-making authority. DDB does this globally, and it was an amazing training ground for me.

When I was doing my research to prepare for the DDB job interview, I learned that DDB was one of the most awarded agencies globally. It is known for smarts and knowledge, and thorough research around its clients and their markets, in tandem with planning and strategy. DDB was an incredibly strategic environment. Not that they neglected the creative side, the people in the agency were just constantly aware of the strategic context of all the creative work that they did.

Most of the brands we partnered with were able to achieve double-digit growth. We made sure that the role of our agency in achieving these results could be monitored and measured, so that we could quantify our contribution. Consulting needs to add value, and that value should be measurable.

Today, I've also noticed that agency offerings are starting to more closely resemble those of business consulting and professional-services firms. As agencies, we do our best work when we are allowed into the tent. When clients trust us with the real issues facing their business, we are better equipped to come up with strategies and tactics that help to address them.

A top-end agency needs to be able to give counsel and to advise on business strategy if we are going to be taken seriously and earn our fees. Glen Lomas is a sharp Brit, who taught me so much, and especially inspired me with his ability to hone in on the essence of a problem and then solve it. Creativity is integral to the process, but it's not the be-all and end-all of the service that agencies provide. The service is solutions.

The way I'm telling the story, it may sound like my time at DDB was systematic, organised and perfectly orchestrated. It wasn't really. I was still flying by the seat of my pants a lot of the time, working it out as I went along. No one – least of all Glen, my mentor – conferred the knowledge and the confidence upon me in some kind of wisdom ceremony. I had to put in the hours of work, meet the people, understand the businesses I was working with, and gain knowledge and confidence through that process. The people of DDB simply created space for me to do that. And they were there whenever I needed guidance or advice to keep me on my growth path.

All of my mentors at the various companies I've worked at have walked the journey with me and helped me to become a man. There have been many of them, and they really opened themselves up, giving me the benefit of their vast experience, while also crediting me for the ideas I was able to contribute, and boosting my confidence in that way.

28

Complicit in each other's success

I HAVE A HUGE SENSE of gratitude when I look back at the mentors and informal life coaches who have helped to build me into who I am today. And I feel obliged to live up to the faith that they have shown in me. If I do not become a good leader, it will be a waste of all those hours of overtime; a waste of the training that those good people ploughed into me. It would also be letting down the industry that has helped to build me.

Whatever success I have attained today is due to every individual I have worked with, every agency I have been inspired by, my managers, my colleagues, the team I have built at DNA ... We're a small industry in South Africa, and we achieve greater success by building each other up, rather than tearing each other down. We're all building something together. I am a product of all the agencies I've worked for. Thanks to the healthy turnover of talent within the industry, most of us have worked in a bunch of agencies, and therefore helped to shape the culture and nature of South African advertising, marketing and communications.

Considering how interwoven our destinies are, and how intimately we work together, how easily our ideas cross-pollinate, and how much we influence each other, we cannot pretend that any one of us sprang fully formed from the earth and created ourselves from scratch. We are each other's thoughts, ideas and dedication made manifest. We compete every day, but we are complicit in each other's success, so we must compete with respect.

I was lucky to be raised to have total respect for my elders and I also have the awareness to know that you cannot risk burning a single bridge in an industry as small and close knit as ours. To this day, I find myself invited to events at my former agencies, where I deliver keynotes and motivational chats whenever they ask me. Recently, I was at MTV delivering a keynote address, despite having left there almost a decade ago. This speaks to an avoidance of burning bridges; it speaks to relationships that are kept alive, nurtured and maintained. I have found a way to do business with pride and confidence and respect for all players. I understand our value to each other. We are collaborators as much as competitors, and we're building an industry together.

From an African cultural perspective, a small agency like ours simply does not go out and immediately compete with our elders, our parents. Like an African child, we just humbly grow in our own time. And like proud parents, the larger, older agencies that we grew out of, they want to see us grow. They want to see us do well. I still communicate with industry legend Nunu Ntshingila-Njeke, now head of Facebook Africa, but once CEO and Chair of Ogilvy.

I had achieved some small success, and she contacted me to

tell me how thrilled she was about it. She was just happy for me and where I had managed to get to. Isn't that amazing? There is no rivalry, no jealousy, no bitterness about what happened in years gone by. Just true, honest generosity of spirit. Nunu was associated with Ogilvy for a long time – and set the world on fire, delivering a business model and an approach that has become the template, the essence of the way advertising agencies work in this country and around the world. That agency has roots that are almost 100 years deep, but they constantly work to be fit for the future.

I could not even compare myself and my small agency to the industry icons. Businesses like Ogilvy, DDB and FCB are my elders, their people have walked this path long before me and, whatever I achieve, I achieve thanks to their inspiration. I'm honoured and grateful to be amongst them today. I'm proud that they think of me as a bit of a protégé, the young man who went out into the world and achieved something.

Around the time I was considering starting an agency of my own, I was looking at the portraits of the Ogilvy board members, all of these people with decades of experience in advertising. I couldn't help thinking that each of them had once been in the position I was in. They had also gained some experience, and found themselves in a situation where they could either start a business, or remain with an established company and plough their experience into helping it grow further. Each of them was a link between the elders who had inspired them, and the next generation, the kids who were going to take up the torch and carry on.

Those board members had decided to stay on with Ogilvy, and had risen to become luminaries. But their contribution to the development of the marketing tradition was colossal. Starting a small agency, or growing a large agency ... these are just different ways to contribute, and each of us in the industry will find ourselves suited to a different approach. We contribute in so many different ways.

While consolidation is certainly a thing, it is not conceivable that we could get to a point where we have one enormous agency serving all the brands on earth. Each brand requires a unique strategy to grow and to succeed and, for each, there will be an agency that is best suited to devising and delivering that strategy. Sure, some brands are mainstream behemoths, perfectly happy with large, global agencies that represent more than 100 clients from a few hundred offices across the world.

But some brands are fresh and young. They are challenging the incumbent big brands in their sectors and they are looking to upset the applecart a little. They are disruptors, and they need disruptor agencies with a similar fearless, anarchic approach. Agencies that are more like them.

There is a system in place that allows us all to work together comfortably. I see the bigger agencies as my parents, but parents of an adult who is now grown and can stand on his own two feet. They have raised a great child, a product of their times, their values and their culture. That child approaches challenges in a similar way to them. Some things, the child cannot hope to do better than the parent. Other things, through a combination of youthful exuberance, energy and sheer, crazy bravado, the child *can* now do better than the parent. I'm proud of the person I've become, and the agency I've built, and my parent agencies can be proud too.

You have to constantly remember where you've come from. At some point in your life you're going to look in the mirror and understand that you're standing in a place you once dreamed of getting to. You're there now, and it's not simply thanks to your own exertions, but because you were carried here, lifted by people who are bigger and stronger than you are. Their roles are every bit as important as yours. Their DNA runs through your veins too. You are the genetic descendant of those who came before you. That idea lives in the name of the agency I started in 2012 ... DNA Brand Architects.

I want to do my mentors justice. I want them to be proud of what they have raised. The work I do through the agency we have been able to build is all part of that.

29

Seedlings in a nursery

THE BEAUTY OF LIVING in the city you grew up in is that, everywhere you go, the spaces evoke stories from your life. For me, Johannesburg is like a physical repository of my memories – the human buzz of Soweto, the inner-city bustle of downtown Jozi, the northern suburbs, where I have spent most of my working life ... When I drive around town, I am constantly reminded of past experiences. It's like driving through my world of memories. Every time I drive through Sandton, I am transported back to my days at the FCB offices. I'm reminded of the legendary office bar and the many hours spent shooting the breeze after work, or playing some kind of quirky office games. The place that was the genesis of my career is still physically present, there to stimulate my memories.

I usually pass the FCB offices on my way out of Sandton, towards Joburg's M1 highway. It takes me back to those glory days, when the future was wide open, our energy was limitless and we still had so much to learn. But what a place to learn it! There, dealing with big clients, big accounts, big brands! Vodacom, Toyota, Tiger Brands … All the big players were open to working with us. We were South Africa's top-rated agency at the time.

————•————

The FCB space produced some incredible thinkers. The 12 of us in our intern cohort were blessed to get the benefit of that thinking – both in its structure and in terms of the ideas themselves. It's common to use the word "nurturing" as a throwaway term. But we were really nurtured, in terms of being reared, supported and raised, like young seedlings in a nursery. We were well looked after, mentored and trained. That was done carefully enough that we have been able to build healthy businesses of our own – a new line in marketing nurseries, if you will. We've infused our learnings into our businesses, into the way we do things at our agencies and spaces.

My time at Ogilvy was marked by the absolute focus on the work. The systems of the business are built around supporting the work, and generating the right outcomes for the clients. Those systems were sometimes rather complex, but they worked.

30

The spirit of change

ANOTHER GEM FROM THE treasure trove of my memories is a short letter from one of my former agencies, telling me that they're so very proud to hear that we had won a major piece of business. It's not the only such letter from them. I constantly felt that I was being elevated and pushed by people who sincerely wanted me to succeed. In a lot of ways, I think of those attitudes as the genesis of true transformation in our country.

The most effective modern companies are those that see black advancement as more than a compliance issue, or a box-ticking exercise. Their concern is with the growth and development of the black child in their care. I believe this is the right way to approach any form of transformation policy. As long as we have the best interests of the beneficiaries at heart, we will see positive outcomes for employment equity programmes. Where transformation takes place reluctantly, or it is done with a resentful heart, the outcomes will be inconsistent. It takes generosity of spirit to achieve real, meaningful change.

A decade and more later, we the interns are now agency owners, CEOs and senior company executives. We are not BEE fat cats, but working professionals, our gains from the transformation process were not financial, but intellectual. We gained knowledge, not tenders, contracts, share options or other financial incentives. What we were given was for the good of the industry, not just for our own personal benefit. My former leaders Nkwenkwe Nkomo and Klasie Wessels are legends, who had the vision to transfer knowledge along with opportunity. We got a foot in the door, and we learned the importance of delivery, excellence, flair, and looking good while you do it. Doing the work, and adding a little sprinkle of magic dust on top.

After that, the celebration of good work in the office just comes naturally. We had consistent, regular Friday celebrations in the office, because we were consistently and regularly doing incredible work that was worth celebrating.

I've learned that you can run on instinct, but at some stage you have to sit down and try to *understand* your instincts. That way, you can channel them at will.

31

How I run the business

THERE IS A CERTAIN glamour to being an agency owner, and at DNA we are known to complement that glamour with a fun "dancing" environment. In everything we do, we try to remember one thing: to stand against bland.

But it's a lot of hard work, and there are also times that are highly unpleasant. Working with a 100 per cent black staff complement is quite something. There is a deep responsibility. Deeper than deep! These are my brothers and sisters who are systematically precluded from this industry. You have to jump in; you have to be right in the mix, fighting for them and with them!

———⋅———

The right people make the right combination of skill and energy.

Over the years I have been so lucky to have recruited some amazing talents who are suited for "The DNA Way". Because there *is* a way we do things – and we understand that is not for everyone.

———

Many have walked through our doors and they have gone on to do amazingly. The foundation we build and the way we do things inspires a sense of belief in oneself and, I must be honest, I know that my team and everyone who has worked at DNA feels unstoppable. They believe they can make it BIG. We instil that sense of achievement here, and at times it has backfired because you have to be able to back it up. It is not just about feelings and words, but skill and output.

———

Where would I be without our DNA All-Stars, who wake up every morning to join me on this mission? And it is not an easy one. There are highs, lows, cheers and screams. It's unforgiving and painful at times. Business is a roller coaster ride, and you will find yourself queuing to do it all again. Being in business is not a regular gig: it requires grit. It needs truth and it needs foresight and a lot of skill – and energy!

———

I am lucky. I have enjoyed longstanding support from people around me who get it. I look back often and I am really honoured to have touched so many lives through this business. Some have come and some have gone but the vision is fully in action. I have a good support structure in the business and it is getting stronger. An owner needs that. The right level of support that I get from Vincent Zondo, who has been with me for five of the seven years of DNA; Cedrick Diphoko, whose growth I have had the joy of witnessing over the last four years; and, oh man!, Monare Matema, who came fresh from university and is now a full-on award-winning PR professional in his own right. Then there is my Connie, who has been a pillar and sister who lives and breathes our business. I also look back at the sparks that have been ignited by this business too. Many All-Stars who have gone on to do amazingly – inspired by what we do and how we do it. These are some of the joys of running a business. You can make a difference, for real!

—•—

Managing people is a psychological undertaking; it takes deep engagement and understanding. That engagement can be incredibly draining and exhausting on a mental and a psychic level.

In a sense, when we manage people, we apply our minds to what the organisation needs and we deploy our colleagues to deliver. At other times, we manage their performances so that they can be better. Another role is to mentor, coach and to train. Where we do that really well, we can also inspire those we work with. On another level, we form deep partnerships; our colleagues bring skills we don't have, perspectives we might not yet have developed. Knowledge of people, places and cultures that are not our strong point. I believe this is vital. If a company is to grow, it needs all kinds of talent, people of all kinds of abilities.

We seek these people out. We determine what we need in our organisation, then we network, we advertise, we interview, and we engage new people, we bring new members into our team. With senior team members, this might take months. We might start our engagement with a friendly coffee meeting. Then we might invite the person over to the office to get a feel for the place, for our vibe. Finally, we might get down to the nitty-gritty, start talking about the role we see for them, what the job description might be, what kind of remuneration might work for both of us. These senior roles are the most delicate, because a senior staff member can have a significant impact on the team dynamic. They are going to be part of shaping our culture, the spirit that drives the organisation, of shaping and mentoring the other team members. As a senior executive, or an agency owner, the decision of who to work with on a senior level is crucial. It takes insight, vision, an incredibly perceptive feel for people and, more than anything else, it takes trust.

———•———

The stakes are high. The right hire can make an exponential difference to your business. But hiring the wrong person can destabilise your operation, negatively impacting everything you do, affecting your people and sometimes taking months and years to correct.

———•———

I am proud of my ability to relate to others, and I think of myself as a good judge of people – you have to be, growing up in the township. The game on the streets is a lot about building alliances and knowing who to trust. Life in business is similar.

But my judgement is far from perfect, and my hiring has not always been flawless. Like most business owners, I have found myself at times with the wrong person in the wrong position. For a positive, nurturing person like myself, who always sees the best in others, this is an incredibly difficult situation. I have not hired this person lightly. I have interviewed them, agonised and then decided they are the right hire for our organisation. Then we have integrated them, brought them right into the bosom of our business, shared our secrets with them, and enlisted their help in shaping the way we will do things going forward. If done fully and with real openness, this is an intimate relationship. We have allowed each other into our inner sanctum, physically and psychologically. To do this, and then to find that you are not a match, can be one of business's bigger disappointments.

As business owners, we operate on instinct and intuition as well as blood, sweat and tears. With a staff problem, after a while that instinct starts to tell you something, and it's important that you listen.

Once you decide there might be a problem, it's time for fact-finding. Speak to as many team members as you can, to get an idea of a possible flaw in the system, and the extent of it. This should be done subtly, and with an open mind. Avoid prejudging the situation. Allow the various perspectives to gradually reveal the *real* situation.

———•———

If you become sure that there is a staff problem within your company, it's time to speak to the individual in question. What I have tended to do is invite them for a talk, to discuss the issues that I have with their performance – as well as any other issues that have come up during the fact-finding process. Once you speak to the person, you will have a better idea of what to do next. They may have a perfectly reasonable explanation for the issues. In this case, your problem is one of communication, which certainly needs to be addressed. Communication within a company should be honest, systematic and regular, so that everyone knows what is going on at all times. The goal, after all, is to align everyone's efforts, and that takes communication.

If the problem is not communication, it may be systemic – related to the structures of your company and the way you do things. If this is the case, it should also be addressed urgently, with the input of staff, management and possibly outside consultants.

Finally, if neither systems nor communication are the problem, it may be the individual. Performance management is the process to follow, identifying the problem, measuring it and providing targets for material improvements. After an agreed time, assess the measurables and report back on whether you feel there has been progress and improvement. This "improvement" should be within the deliverables of the staff member, and across their sphere of influence in the organisation. If, within a reasonable time, they are not doing better, and your company is suffering because of it, it is time to start a disciplinary process.

Disciplining a colleague is a nasty business, which no one enjoys. However, it is a crucial part of your toolkit as a manager and an entrepreneur. It's not all love, light and positivity in the business world. Our organisations need maintenance and adjustment as we grow, and we should be prepared to make the changes necessary to ensure everyone – staff, clients, suppliers, investors, communities – continue to benefit from us being in business.

We are all complex beings, and we bring our own issues and characteristics with us when we go to work for a company. When a person's issues start to affect the company, the company needs to take steps to help that person. If the person is unwilling or unable to participate in this process, it is probably time for you to part ways.

I have been through this process a few times with people who have worked with me. I find it highly unpleasant, as it conflicts with my personality. I tend to see the best in everybody, and when someone messes up, I'm generally willing to give them another chance. If someone's explanation for something sounds fishy, I usually give them the benefit of the doubt, but that is in my social life. In my business, I have to be firmer. If you start damaging my company, and the livelihood of all of us who depend on the business, I cannot just give you the benefit of the doubt. I must address it and, if the damage continues, you're going to have to leave us.

Whether that "leaving" involves your resigning or being dismissed, the process will take its course. People who behave unethically are like a cancer in an organisation. The disease spreads and infects the people it touches. The culture and the morale of your enterprise suffers. Working with a demotivated or cynically unethical individual will make their colleagues either embrace their negative values, or become demotivated themselves. They will look to management to address the problem and, if they see no sign of that, they will start investigating ways of leaving the company. That is where "giving someone the benefit of the doubt" can get you. Sure, keep an open mind about suspicions of wrongdoing, but investigate. And if you find evidence, act!

These are the practicalities of performance management. However, I will be the first to admit to the tremendous psychological toll they take on everybody involved. Someone whose performance is being managed goes through an incredibly stressful period. They are being asked to significantly improve their performance, to meet new standards. This means they must either accept the challenge and work harder and better, or they must leave the company.

The manager, or business owner overseeing this disciplinary process, in partnership with the staff member and the human resources department, also goes through a lot. Like the five stages of grief mentioned in the Kubler-Ross model, the business owner confronted with an unethical individual in their company experiences it in several stages. At first you deny it's happening, you close your ears, and you overlook what others might see as obvious signs. When someone explains it away, you take their word for it. Aware of the psychological labour it will take, you postpone investigating the complaints. Then you convince yourself that you need to take action, and the process starts. As in the case of a grieving person, you also find yourself experiencing anger, bargaining, depression and acceptance.

Another emotion I have experienced is a sense of betrayal. After all, this is a person I have trusted with some of my company's most valuable secrets, I have accepted them into my work family and enlisted their help in building a culture and a business. To learn that this person has been undermining that trust is deeply hurtful, disappointing and disturbing. It undermines that confidence, instinct and intuition that drives so many of the best businesses. If you've experienced this, you'll know the feeling. If you trusted this person, you thought they were so good, and they turn out to be such a rotten apple, then can you trust your instincts about *other* parts of the business? What if some of your other colleagues are undermining you, whether by dishonesty, malice, incompetence, laziness or complacency?

These feelings of betrayal are part of running a business. Feel them, learn from them. Use the lessons you learn to ensure it does not happen again.

When you don't move to address a negative assault on your company's culture, your team begins to accept it. They start thinking, "Well, this is how we do things around here."

I get chills when I think back to the handful of traumatic disciplinary events I've had to go through. What shocked me about some of them is that everyone thought it was okay:

this outrageous, unethical behaviour was starting to become accepted!

"Why didn't you tell me?" I asked, but the perception was already taking root that this was acceptable – especially if management weren't yet doing anything to actively discourage it.

When this starts to happen, a first instinct is sometimes to blame yourself. After all, this is a business that I created, I remember thinking. How could I let this happen? I have been incredibly disappointed with myself at these times. When I uncover behaviour that is wrong in every way, in my own space – it's hard not to take that kind of thing personally. On another level, it's acceptable to be a bit overwhelmed. Sometimes you slip into a cycle of asking, "Why?" Why did this person do what they did? Sometimes it's useful to let that go. You may never know exactly why they did what they did. It's impossible to understand all of it.

The best response to being let down in business is to follow all legal and labour regulations to a tee. Combat a disregard for the rules with an honest respect for the law. Give the person every opportunity to improve, and ensure that all of their rights are respected.

Do you close your eyes, Harvey Weinstein-style, and pretend like nothing has happened? Of course not! You have to be quite tough. Sooner or later, the person in question will respond. They will either significantly improve their behaviour, or they will have to leave. Often, their deciding to resign is the best for all concerned. When this happens, it can be such a relief.

But you're not out of the woods yet. If the process of managing a particular staff member is "damage control", the real task is *repairing* the damage and ensuring it doesn't recur. This is a culture job. You must re-emphasise everything you stand for as an organisation, and communicate those values effectively to your staff. You must live those values too, visibly and consistently, to ensure your statements of mission and purpose are more than just words.

Relationships may have to be repaired – internally and externally. Balance must be restored, and new team members hired.

There must also be time for some personal healing. That's certainly been my experience. But once my own healing is done, I still wish the best for the person I have parted ways with. I mean what I say about not burning bridges in our industry. Even people I have separated with for work reasons ... I try to find a way to repair our relationships. Barring some really deep ethical differences, we should still be prepared to greet and be civil to each other. We are all humans trying to live our lives, wrestling our own personal demons along the way.

32

My people

WHERE WOULD WE BE without the people that fuel our fire and keep us honest and on track? I am not talking about people around you, for fancy parties or cool events, I am talking about people who are there for you, not for what they get from you, but because they dig you and because, deep down, your success is theirs.

My family has been a light and they have let me live my truth. In that way, they have empowered me to be my best – to find confidence and to be able to express my energy without feeling out of place.

Everyone needs a friend who can cut through the clutter and give it to you straight and I have been lucky to walk almost two decades with my bestie Wilco Muthige, who I call "Dee". He has been there through most of it. We have recorded albums, travelled every township in the country so we can say "we have been there", drunk every new cider on the market, danced up a storm at Simply Blue, Liquid Blue, Europa, you name it. We have jotted down ideas and have seen some of those ideas manifest.

At our usual catch up over a glass of cheap wine and chow mein back in 2006, I told him about the idea of DNA Brand Architects and what I was thinking and, since then, we have spoken about it every week – we still do! Every time he visits my office, he looks at me with such pride and I get teary. We did it, friend! Dee is my bestie, my brother, my confidant, my therapist, my comedian and my business coach. What a joy!

Then I get home, to one of the most amazing human beings I have ever met. Tumelo Mmusi is the wind beneath my wings – my "huzz" – constantly reminding me that our home is not DNA and that our three poodles are not DNA All-Stars. "You are not the CEO here!", he choons me straight. He inspires me to be great. I am valued here; I am my most vulnerable, and every single morning the cup of coffee he makes for me reminds me that I hit the jackpot!

People who love and care for you don't just sing your praises, they challenge you. They give you different perspectives and, more importantly, they keep you on track. They keep you honest. Many times it sucks because, as they say, the truth hurts. But your people know how to push you to be your best.

The tribe makes life colourful and I appreciate the value they bring to my life experience. I think of it as a triangle. One point is you, the other is a close partner and the other is a friend. They create what I call a zone of magic. It's positively challenging, it's vulnerable, it's supportive, there is mad love in it and it is fun!

33

Shut up and be grateful

SOME OF MY MOST important growth experiences have been unpleasant at the time, but they have strengthened me. My difficult times have given me added respect for the leaders of the biggest companies. I was certainly hurt at the time my problems occurred. But today, you will never hear me moaning about how painful some of my business setbacks were.

Once the pain has passed, it's the learnings that have stayed with me. They have been immense. My learnings have led me to create a completely new set of structures in my company. Today, our communication is clearer, our relationships are more honest and our systems more efficient – and we're always looking for ways to improve. Our toughest experiences have made the business better. There have been a few tough times, and there will be more in the future, but you are not defined by your setbacks. You are defined by how you respond to them.

You cannot let them defeat you. It's natural to want to wallow in it sometimes, to feel sorry for yourself. But you need to change, to become better. If you can do that, and you can prove it to yourself, then you'll be able to achieve anything. Remember the dark valleys you have to pass through, because one day, you'll conquer mountains again, and you'll be able to tap yourself on the shoulder and say, "Hey, look down there. Look how far we've come!"

My character-building experiences have given me so much more confidence in my ability to manage a crisis. Now I know that I can face an external challenge to my business. I can face any internal challenges that might arise. They don't teach that in business school. The only school with that on the curriculum is the School of Going Through It.

"Take lessons from your hardships" sounds like the stuff of motivational books, right? But the truth is that life is hard. We don't operate in a perfect system. We're not always going to get a fair break, and Donald Trump is the President of the United States. Life could be a lot better right now, but we need to go through it.

Today is a weird time. Being able to understand that is helpful. I am an optimist, but I temper that with realism. It's only when we expect life to be consistently fabulous that we get disappointed. The system is not geared to favour us. It will never ever be perfect. No business person can expect to run an enterprise without facing challenges, toxic situations and serious setbacks. Whether you're Sim Tshabalala, Adrian Gore, Maria Ramos, Dominic Sewela, Elon Musk or Mark Zuckerberg, you are going to have to face some steep uphills – and you will have to overcome!

But nothing is ever so bad that it couldn't be a lot worse. You might be battling corruption inside your organisation, or a hostile takeover, or an employee double-invoicing or stealing a client, but on the other side of town, an entrepreneur is folding the company they've been running for 20 years. In another industry, a large bank is laying off 2 000 people or makes a loss of a staggering $1.3 billion due to a bad acquisition. That is a challenge of an entirely different order. It helps to keep that kind of perspective.

Whatever we're going through, there are people who are dealing with far bigger issues than ours. A simple look at the headlines in the news will contextualise things quite quickly. When I compare my small struggles to the decisions that the CEOs of some big companies have to make, I quickly realise I need to just shut up and be grateful.

34

What makes a leader

I LIKE TO THINK of myself as a leader. If I'm going to be worthy of the name, I need to forget the ego. I need to be able to humble myself and say, "I'm sorry for anything that I've done that may have hurt you". Having the ability to apologise and to start the healing makes for better humans and better leaders. If we're going to hold each other accountable, we need to hold ourselves to the same standard.

We can't build a stronger society if everyone just does whatever they want. What applies in our business microcosm must apply across our country. I expect people to be held accountable on a national scale, so the same principles must apply on a small-business scale. In private enterprises, the risks of irresponsible behaviour are even more significant, with little built-in reporting, and no public scrutiny.

As a business owner, in a sense you are the ultimate leader

of your organisation. Your word is law. If your operation is not big enough to have to account to a board or to a shareholder, you can start to feel omnipotent. There is no one to stop you running matters exactly the way you want, and no one is going to hold you to account. We often talk about how we despise dictatorships, but it's possible to build a dictatorship of your own within your business.

If your company becomes a dictatorship and the business goes off the rails due to poor decisions and a lack of consultation, that will be your fault, as the business owner. You should be holding yourself to account; you should have built systems that *force* you to account. Sadly, the world is not a democratic space by nature. Often the strongest, the ones with the most power, will dominate. And so it is within a business.

Even CEOs of listed companies can fall into this trap. Often, they are deeply experienced, with real knowledge of their sector, and it becomes tempting for them to disregard the opinions of others and to forge ahead using their own judgement. Where does independence and self-sufficiency slip through into bloody-mindedness and authoritarianism? No one will know, unless checks and balances are built into the company structure to limit concentration of power.

I've met enough senior execs and business owners to know that there are some unique risks at the top of large organisations – material, financial and spiritual too. The individuals who occupy those rarified heights, the C-suites and the corner offices – those are some fascinating individuals. Each has developed their methods of coping with those risks, the stresses, the temptations, the soul-destroying disappointments.

The very best of them have that ability to prioritise. There it is again. It's a shrewd business tactic and a method of self-preservation. You can only do a finite amount, so start with whatever's most important.

People like you and me might struggle a bit with the harder-edged aspects of this business. We're relaxed; we like to spread happiness; we're sensitive. But a part of that sensitivity is doing what's necessary, even if it's not a pleasant undertaking.

35

What drives you

My time at DDB was spent working with some really experienced professionals. They inspired me and helped to chisel me into shape as a marketing strategist. My passion may have started earlier, but the hard skills and the self-belief came at DDB. By the time I left there, I was the finished product. And I was still getting better. I had learned so much more. "Maybe I'm getting good at this," I thought to myself.

That was confidence, a key part of success. Self-belief.

When you spend several years doing something, and picking up various ancillary skills, you become far more aware of what is possible. That's where that sense of confidence comes from. I absolutely loved working at DDB. But, as with all types of work, there are cycles. You spend a few years building up a track record and getting more experience. After a while, you find yourself with a client in a similar situation to one you've faced before. That's lucky, because you know what your options are, and which decisions to make. At the same time, you're like, "Hang on, I've seen this situation before. What's new?"

That yearning for new challenges is common to many of us. As humans, we like to keep learning, and repeating the same tasks can be unfulfilling for us.

DDB at the time was one of the most exciting, rewarding environments I could have hoped for. There were a bunch of really varied, fascinating jobs in the system at any particular time. I would get to perform in several roles in a short period. Over my time there, I worked on hundreds of campaigns for multiple companies, multiple brands. A brand manager at a corporate might work on only a handful of campaigns, for the same brand, with only subtle variations within the brand narrative. Compared to this, taking briefs from a dozen clients at a time, with all the different challenges that presents, is a rare privilege. I did not take that for granted, but still …

We were working highly effectively, at a fast pace. In these roles, you get to extend your knowledge base very quickly. That is agency life. It's also a double-edged sword, because the deadlines keep coming, work is piling up, and it's possible to get burnt out. I've seen it happen, and no one is immune. Even the most driven, creative people can start to lose that spark of originality they once found so easy to conjure up. People lose that. Some say that five years in an agency is like 50 years in any other kind of company. To survive and keep going, you need to find a way to keep that freshness, commitment and passion alive.

That enthusiasm for your field is what fuels you. It is sacred, and you need to respect it. It is love for what you do. It's all very well to take it for granted, and to think you can summon up ideas and inspiration at will. But it pays to try to understand your mojo, your muse, whatever it is that drives you to perform at your best in your industry. When you start running low on inspiration – which does happen – understanding what drives you will help you to reconnect with it when you need to.

What is it that first drove you to enter your field? What did you love about it? What about it first caught your eye and made you think you could make a career in that space? Think about these questions, and remember your answers. You may need to remind yourself about them from time to time. You need to keep those feelings sacred. Protect that which is beloved to you. That's not always easy in this kind of business.

It can be one of the most heart-breaking parts of working in this industry to feel your love for it start to be eroded. It has happened to me. I recognised it, and I took action to ensure I stayed excited about what I was doing. This industry found me poor, and it provided a career for me. I love working here. It's a job, but it fascinates me, keeps me searching, solving problems for people in creative ways. By and large, I'm always excited to come to work. But I'm constantly on guard against feelings of boredom, or challenges that are not stimulating enough. If I find myself churning out the same old solutions, or client needs stop evolving, I take time to reflect. Advertising and brand communications should not be about the same old solutions.

When it is, it can become deeply frustrating and challenging. At times like that, I do what I can to shake things up, to make the work interesting again. We add new elements, we change the way we work, and we make proactive suggestions to clients about how to invigorate their messaging and their interaction with their audience. Or we find new clients.

In pop psychology, they talk about that "new-relationship energy" that is sparked when we find a new romantic partner. There is something similar in the advertising industry. I once had a meeting with a new client. Their brand is part of the most boring category you could imagine. But, for some reason, it felt like something new and interesting. As we discussed the client's goals, I knew I would be learning something new. And just like that, I felt the magic spark within me. That feeling is why I got into marketing: that thrill of new challenges, new learnings, new ideas.

This incredible industry keeps doing that to you. It keeps throwing up fresh opportunities. The key is to allow yourself to grab them.

At FCB and Ogilvy, the trend was to help develop staff with experience in particular sectors by creating specialty teams that focused on particular disciplines. At DDB we didn't have the luxury of a large staff complement. It was all hands on deck, and we all worked on everything.

Throughout all this time as an employee at these great agencies, my entrepreneurial impulses grew. I was always fascinated by the bigger picture of where my work fitted into the company's business model and its own strategic goals in the marketing industry. How were we managing our people? What was our culture like? If it was amazing, stimulating, motivating and all that good stuff, how did it become like that? Corporate structure and culture fascinated me, because these are the factors that make for highly effective companies.

An agency like Ogilvy has a distinctive culture of its own, which drives its ability to create powerful work for clients. Learning that culture, learning to fit in and operate within it, was a great lesson. Even if the culture wasn't a natural fit for me as an individual, I embraced the chance to understand the ways of this stupendously successful company, now with something like 132 offices in 83 countries.

———•———

With DNA Brand Architects, we've applied some of those

learnings while building a culture uniquely our own, as a young, African agency, for brands with an unstoppable hunger for greatness! We are building a new culture. This process is exciting, even while it's frustrating. A new company must have its own soul; you can't cut-and-paste that from somebody else's playbook. We're building something quite unique with our agency.

One has to work hard to create culture. It starts from values, and purpose. This is what tribes have done since time immemorial. Groups of people unite around an idea, something that binds various individuals together; gives them a shared vision. That vision is what motivates them to apply their thoughts, their energy and their labours in service of the group. The principle applies equally to agencies. We are a tribe of sorts. An African tribe, certainly. We have a vision for bringing a contemporary African take to strategy, reputation management, brand management, content creation and public relations; for doing brand communications in a relevant, contemporary style and creating amazing customer experiences.

Our agency's culture hasn't just come from me. Like the agency itself, our staff growth, our client relationships and the work we've done, the agency's culture has evolved. When you start a business, you do imagine what you would like your culture to be, but culture is a human, living feeling. It must be allowed to grow – the best you can hope for is to be able to shape it along the way. Values, you can try to codify and reinforce, but culture is alive.

Starting out, I wanted to create a space where people would bring their true selves to work, where they would feel open to creating interesting work and inspired to give great service to clients. The space and the culture needed to be different to anything elsewhere in the industry. In designing the space and the systems, I took references from my own experiences at previous workplaces. I reflected on what worked and what didn't work in those environments and used those insights to create better spaces and methods in my own company.

In terms of setting a vision for where I wanted the business to go, I certainly had my goals and my plans for getting there. But the "how", the way we were going to get there, and what we would be like as we got there ... that was down to our people. I could rent the office and fill the space with furniture and design the look and the feel, but then you have people coming into that space, and it takes on a life of its own.

<hr>

Building an operating system for your business is more structured. Workflows and divisional organisation must be effective, clear and easy to understand for everyone, so that we can align our work in service of our clients' goals.

If I have been flexible and laissez-faire about how culture develops in the business that I started, I have been far more hands-on in building the operational systems. I know exactly how I would like things to work in my business. That is part of our unique offering, and it must be consistently reinforced and communicated to the team. At times, a new hire might bring in a work habit from their previous agency, and I'll quickly remind them that it works slightly differently here.

Building culture is the job of everyone in a space. Culture is lived, but it's lived slightly differently for the different people inside that culture. As long as there's a framework that we all understand and relate to, we can grow and develop our culture the way that makes sense to us.

In communicating our core values as a new company, I knew we could not impose a lengthy mission statement on people. The practical way to get everyone on the same page is to distil our motivating principles down to just a handful of ideas.

Energy, values, and people are what it boiled down to for DNA. Those were our priorities, and we set about finding people who naturally shared the same values. We certainly try to find people who fit in with our values, but once they're in, our culture will evolve with their contributions, their personality and their character.

Another focus for us is skill: we need to have the right skills to be able to deliver a suitable calibre of work for our clients. Energy is what will power that. Values, skill and energy became the three founding pillars on which our company was built. Alongside that trio, the people are what make it all real. They bring the skills and the values to life. We don't hire automatons who just do what they're told. We look for strong personalities, people with a hopeful, positive outlook on life. These kinds of people tend to be intelligent and well presented. Like us.

36

Casting for crew

OUR INTERVIEW PROCESS more closely resembles a casting than a job interview.

We cast for team members who will add to the environment. By this stage, seven years into the agency's life, we have built something, and we look for people who will take our project forward in a way we all believe in.

Our recruitment process is very enthusiastically run by our human resources department. People who have helped to build an organisational culture become invested in it. They're protective, and they want to work with like-minded people who share similar values and can share their visions for the company.

We hold castings for those people. Can we see them in the role? Working in our environment is not for everybody. Certain types of people would completely rebel against our culture and our way of doing things. That's fine – the key is for us to make that determination during the interview – and casting – process. Luckily, our HR team has this process on lock. They know what they're doing, so I just leave them to it. I'm not an HR person. By this stage, I'm more of a business operations manager.

But the people come to us! The beauty of building a brand and establishing yourself in your industry is that if you do it right, people will come to understand your values and those who share them will naturally gravitate towards you. In the same way I decided while I was still in UJ lectures that I wanted to work at FCB, young media professionals today gravitate towards DNA. We have built a critical mass of culture, which has its own gravity and attracts the right people to us. People now know what we stand for, they know what we're looking for in our recruits, and it's quite easy to see if someone is a DNA person, which makes our interviews relatively quick. But values, skill and energy will be the attributes we look for in all our candidates. That's what we believe will serve us as we grow into the future.

Another attribute we look for in a business like ours is a person with an inner calm. You need to be centred, in a spiritual sense, if you're going to survive the changing nature of our industry. They need creative thinking, because we're not in the business of simply putting A into B.

Another indispensable character strength is the ability to grow. I believe that growth should not stop at any point in our lives. Communication today is not stagnant, so there is no need for stagnant personalities! We embrace new developments and combine them, we don't specialise in one particular stream of doing things. The world is changing, and our people are open to it.

It's useful to think what your values are. If you were an agency, and you had to emblazon a handful of core values on a neon sign in the lobby of your business, what would that sign say? What would you want to remind people about every time they came to see you? What would you stand for?

If you're running a company, do you already know what those values are? Are you communicating them clearly to your team and to your clients? If you're an individual, and you were asked, could you identify the three core values that you stand for? If you went into a job interview now, would you be able to articulate your principles clearly and concisely, so that you and your potential bosses could quickly tell whether you would be a good fit?

37

The skills of the future

SKILLS ARE ANOTHER attribute that must constantly evolve. The skills that are required for the future are not the same traditional group of skills that have served us as a species until this point. In the future, it won't be all science, maths, engineering and geography. What our evolving social and business environment is likely to demand are interdisciplinary skills.

We will obviously still need specialists, but there will also be a need for "deep generalists", people with a knowledge of various fields and the ability to tie them all together with a holistic perspective.

Emotional intelligence will also be critical. In a world where more and more tasks will become automated, humans will have fewer repetitive tasks. In order to still be useful – in the corporate environment and to society at large – we will need to develop abilities that favour our humanity. Our humanity cannot be replicated by artificial intelligence or machine learning – at least not at this stage.

Sense-making will be another handy future skill – the ability to determine the deeper meaning of what is being expressed.

Social intelligence will be a crucial attribute. Similar to emotional intelligence, it's the ability to connect to others in a deep and direct way, especially in a group context. People with social intelligence are able to sense and stimulate reactions from others and also to bring about the right kinds of interactions with others.

If we're going to distinguish ourselves from computers, we will also need adaptive thinking – the ability to find solutions that are not rule-based.

On a social level, the future will require cross-cultural competency. This is something we're fairly familiar with in South Africa – code-switching and being able to operate in different cultural settings.

We'll also need to be able to interpret data, to develop our ability to translate vast amounts of information into insights.

Finally, we will need the skill of load management, or prioritising. That old chestnut. As we become bombarded with data from our growing number of information systems, we need to be able to filter it, and distinguish the data sets that are most important to us. People of the future will need to be able to prioritise their tasks. In a time when anything is possible, what will you choose to do?

38

The call of the bird

I ONLY SPENT THREE years at DDB. But they were three intense years of developing my superpowers, in a way. Looking back, it feels like I was there a lot longer, because I was working so hard. I was busy, and I grew phenomenally. I would have stayed longer, but Nando's gave me a call.

There was a headhunter who knew about me. I guess I had started to make some waves in the industry beyond my organisation. I had won the odd award and been asked to speak at some events, which is where the headhunter met me. Then one day, she called.

"There's a role you'd be perfect for," she said. "You need to go and meet these guys."

"Who is it for?"

"Nando's."

At the time, my first thought was, oh Lord, it's a restaurant.

The idea of working at a chain of restaurants – even if it was the leading international food chain from South Africa – just didn't feel sexy to me. I was sceptical, but the more I thought about it, the more I realised that this was really one of South Africa's most exciting brands. Nando's was fresh, brave, proudly South African – and looking at its rapid growth, it was clearly a well-run company. From humble beginnings with a single store in Rosettenville, Nando's had grown to where it had hundreds of outlets in territories from Canada to the UK, UAE to Australia. I decided to make that phone call.

The minute I met the team, I knew that we would be able make it work. Their interview process was also similar to casting for a production, in a lot of ways. Meeting the people is about chemistry and values, shared values. I could feel that I would be led to bigger achievements.

People can only be their best in environments where they feel comfortable, spaces where they can be who they really are. When I walked into Nando's, I felt completely at ease, completely myself. I had my first meeting with Teresa Mordoh, a technical marketer who understood the skills and requirements for the role. I must have got the green light from her, because my next meeting was with Kevin Utian, the CEO. Yes, he of the unforgettable "are you gay?" question.

Well, we know how that interview ended.

I left the meeting, and received a call back a short while later.

"You've got the job," said the voice on the other end of the line. "We want you to be our new national marketing manager."

My time at Nando's was an amazing experience. It was a test of character on many fronts, but I passed all of those tests.

Nando's isn't the kind of place where you just walk in and start telling people what to do. There is an established method of operating. Franchisees are a bunch of strong characters, and vital to the business. I needed to win their confidence, and learn from them, if we were going to work together effectively. Doing that was an interesting experience for me, and a test of my social intelligence.

The first significant difference I noticed, coming from my agency background, was a new understanding of brand. At an agency, one might work on 20 brands at one time. You give them each all the focus you can, but this is not on the same deep, all-embracing level you get to when you are representing just one brand. At an advertising agency, you are serving a brand. In the corporate environment, you *are* the brand. This was to be my first time representing a brand at that level. The last time I had represented a brand exclusively had been back when I was looking after the Verimark stand on weekends!

I was arriving at a business known for creating amazing work, and I was tasked with reinvigorating the brand. Fortunately, there was a legacy of incredible marketing success to take inspiration from and to build upon. Nando's was already iconic in South African marketing. The brand had been named one of the world's hottest marketing brands. On the awards circuit, they had been winning accolades for years, especially during their partnership with TBWA\Hunt\Lascaris. That agency had helped to infuse the brand with a unique personality – cheeky and irreverent – that was also quintessentially South African.

We chose Black River FC to partner with us on the next stage of the Nando's adventure. That agency had exactly what we needed at the time: an edgy, cheeky, iconoclastic attitude, and the energy to pull it off.

It was the start of an amazing trip. To this day, I absolutely adore that agency. Working with them was a jam, and a pleasure! If I were launching a new brand today, I would want to work with them again. They just *get* it. The people at Black River FC, Ahmed Tilly and his team, they just understand what's going on.

The challenge was real. Nando's was looking to bring a

fresh, eye-catching and inspiring angle to its campaigns that also needed to drive the bottom line and sell meals for the franchisees.

I was not there to simply push the brief. I also had to inspire – internally and externally. I had to work with the agency to get the messaging to just the right level. This meant creative excellence, edgy, memorable ads and promotions that worked. This was a difficult balancing act, but it made for challenging and rewarding work.

Because I came from an agency background, it was expected that I would immediately understand the brand. Luckily, I was able to school myself up quite quickly. I was familiar with client-agency engagement, so I was quickly able to build a beautiful relationship with Black River. I understood exactly what the dynamics were, and how to get the best work out of the agency. It requires motivating in a particular manner. This was my first time on the opposite end of that relationship, and that made me reevaluate the fundamentals. What does the client really need in an agency? From the agency perspective, what is the best way to deliver on client needs?

At the core of it, the client wants the best work from an agency. To them, this supports the bottom line. Awards are nice to have, but the strategic purpose of marketing is to drive business. Creative, inspiring, fulfilling work is often an agency priority, which can make them lose sight of the sales imperatives.

The client's follow-up question after being shown a potentially award-winning campaign is always, "But will it drive sales?"

Will it drive sales, volumes, online consideration and purchase, or whatever metrics the client is using to measure success? It's a rare company that states one of its goals at their annual marketing conference as "We want to win more advertising awards"! It's always about sales.

If you meditate on it a bit longer, you come to understand that, at the core, the jobs are the same. Client and agency are working together to help meet the client's business objectives. But in trying to achieve that, you need to manage people in appropriate ways. I was in the lucky position of being able to understand what it would take to get the agency to do the best, most effective work, but in a way that they were happy with and proud of. It wasn't a zero-sum game – we could have it all! Fulfilling, award-winning campaigns that sold chicken in Port Elizabeth, Witbank, Maponya Mall, and every Nando's outlet in the country!

At Nando's, it became crucial to ensure our internal and outside-facing systems were flawless. I needed to know that all the levers I had set up to ensure great work were working correctly. Teresa Mordoh and soon after that Julian Bryant were instrumental in this regard.

Business happens in a complex, ever-shifting social environment. We are subject to the ebbs and flows of current affairs. Sentiment, external shocks, a broader narrative … Sometimes, great campaigns will deliver great sales, and other times, because of these broader factors, it just won't happen. It would be simplistic to essentialise the equation to "great marketing equals great sales". But subject to that understanding, at the core of it, "great work works".

As a marketer, I understand this implicitly. I'm actually not interested in doing work that is not going to push anything forward. As part of the team working on a client's account, you want to drive the business. This was especially so at Nando's, where some of the edgiest campaigns would come out, and I would have the whole company looking at me going, "Well let's hope it works."

I was part of an incredible team of people. But because of the brand aspect, I often found myself at the forefront of consumer relations. At one point, I was The Nando's Guy. This kind of complete brand commitment can be a challenge to deal with, especially for someone with an agency history. It can feel like the brand is filtering into your identity. Other people define you in terms of the brand, and it can become difficult to separate where your brand personality ends, and your private personality begins. I certainly experienced this.

At first it upset me. I felt unacknowledged for my personal attributes, as if everything I was was due to the brand. Even in the time after leaving Nando's, I still find myself associated with that brand. I've since been able to make peace with this, and even to be grateful. The truth is, I'm proud to be associated with the brand. It was an incredible company to work for, and it taught me a lot. I was the marketing manager at Nando's at an important time in its history – what a privilege!

People know the name. That's something to work with, and if I get some shine from being related to that brand, I am most grateful. I know I've proved myself independently as well, but I will never regret being associated with Nando's. In South Africa's small marketing environment, this conflation of spokespeople, ambassadors and influencers with the brand they represent is common. Sure, it might be difficult to convince people that you no longer work there, but hey! At least there is something that connects you to these people.

I am still humbled by this kind of recognition. It's not always positive, though. You might be celebrated for the brand's successes, but you will also be called upon to account for perceived brand missteps. You have to take everything that sticks to you!

For a long time, I was "Sylvester from Nando's", and to a lot of people I still am. I was on a radio show recently, where a caller had an epiphany when they realised I was *that* Sylvester. I gently reminded them that I'm no longer there.

The impact that brand has had on my life has been phenomenal. To be part of the Nando's leadership was a true privilege. To work with Kevin Utian, the CEO; Robbie Brozin, who founded the company; Paul Appleton, who was the group chief marketing director on the international side ...

I went to school all over again at that company, and they were my teachers. They ploughed themselves into my growth. They gave me wings!

———•———

Nando's gave me a platform. As I had been at DDB, I was empowered. I could make decisions and I could get things done. Now, I also had the power of a local-but-international brand behind me.

Having authority is not for a marketing manager to take for granted. In some companies, a marketing manager must make a budget request to their bosses for any extra initiative. But I had a fair bit of latitude. Nando's understood that for a company to really get the best out of its team, the team needed to have the power to decide and implement on its own. This encourages initiative. At Nando's the attitude is, "Great idea! Go and do it!"

If an executive has to consult right across the company before they can launch any new project, it slows down innovation, and also undermines confidence. Many businesses might pay lip service to empowering their people, but will fail to really trust them. It's almost like they want their chief marketing officer to make all the decisions. This creates such a bottleneck, because every new idea means a request and motivation must be prepared and this all needs to be considered by the same person. A culture of empowerment removes the bottlenecks and allows everyone in the organisation to start driving and implementing good ideas.

Nando's wasn't a walk in the park. But being trusted and empowered affected my leadership style. It gave me the confidence to win over the franchisees. The franchisees are invested in the success of the company in more ways than one. They insist that every cent of marketing spend is accounted for, and they want to see results! We would go out on roadshows across South Africa to tell the Nando's franchisees about our latest campaigns. This was an internal marketing job in a parallel quest to market chicken to consumers. On those roadshows, you had to make sure those guys understood the campaign, liked it and saw how it was going to support their businesses. Some of them were tough nuts to crack – no-nonsense, salt-of-the-earth guys who just wanted to know how this clever campaign was going to sell them more chicken.

This is corporate life. You need to have an internal and external focus if you're going to keep the company aligned. You're lobbying to make sure that people believe in you. Making sure that people hear about your successes so it will be easier to get them on board for the next project. Any slip-ups, and I would get grilled (pardon the pun) for not having delivered on particular elements or objectives. We were spending franchisees' money on those campaigns, and we were never allowed to forget that. Franchisees were paying us – with a portion of their franchise fees – to market their businesses. We were only custodians of that budget.

Working together helped us get to know each other better, and we soon developed an understanding. Through roadshows and screen presentations, we were able to bring all members of the Nando's family into our confidence and get them to buy into our strategy. Session by session, roadshow by roadshow, we got to a space where we were respected and heard. It didn't happen overnight. I worked damn hard to get people to believe in me. But it was achieved. I had moved out of the sometimes-insular agency space, into the real world of retail and restaurants. I gained confidence from being able to make a success of that, and from the constant support I got from my colleagues and my seniors.

"We believe in you," they would tell me from time to time. "Keep going."

The level of encouragement, support and endorsement that I received at Nando's is still precious to me. I know what it means to have your ability respected implicitly, to be trusted and to have the freedom to be a leader in your area. Because I so appreciate that I was given this in my career, I strive to do the same for the managers who work with me.

It's great to be empowered, but, as they say, with great power comes great responsibility. Not every project will go your way. And when it doesn't, you have to learn to take responsibility. There's also a constant pressure to deliver. One massive failure, and all that trust and confidence can be lost. You also don't want to let down the people who have shown faith in you. They are also taking a career risk in pinning their hopes on you, the youngest person in the entire set-up. There's a new kid on the block and they're telling everybody, "Don't worry, we can believe in him."

They're taking a risk, and it's another massive responsibility not to betray the faith they've shown in you, or to disappoint them.

I've always been among the youngest people in most of my work environments. Perhaps I was a bit of a young achiever, but I was always cognisant of not wanting to come across as too young. A lot of the feedback I received on my leadership style at that point was that I was perhaps overcompensating for my youth. I was young, and I was desperate to be taken seriously, so I was being too serious at times.

Already at Nando's, energy was something I believed in. There has to be a positive energy at the core of what you're doing. At that point in my life, denying my youth was like denying my energy I was limiting myself. In trying to seem more mature, I was bottling up a lot of my youthful strength, stamina and enthusiasm. The work itself was certainly challenging, and worth being taken seriously. But we can't allow the work to turn us into old people! As I grew into the job, I learned to lighten up and to relax. I was young, but I could do the job, and people respected that.

Today, as an entrepreneur, I'm serious about my job. It's my life, and I'm engaged in a process of trying to grow something. But there is a balance I've learned to strike so that I'm able to have fun with it. If we don't season our hard work with fun, life becomes bland. Learning to do that has helped me a lot. Taking a lighter approach to life also helps me recharge, so that I'm better able to deal with the real challenges when they arrive. If I'm in a fun, positive, enthusiastic place, when faced with a crisis, I'm up for it.

So, I lived my truth as an energetic young, black gay man, and it worked. At one stage at Nando's, I was rocking a ginger mohawk hairstyle. I mean, it was ridiculous. I guess I pushed the dial all the way to 10 on the Youthful Enthusiasm scale. When I look at the pictures now, I want to die! A mohawk, T-shirt and jeans. That's the way we dressed back then, whether we were on a Nando's roadshow on the *platteland* or going for meetings in Washington DC.

39

Work that wins friends

IT'S A COMMON marketing cliché to say that "the work is everything." But it holds a lot of truth. What really shifted my profile at Nando's was a campaign that we did with an agency called Stick Communications to coincide with the 2009 national elections. It was a controversial campaign, and I ended up becoming the spokesperson for it when things went south.

Stick were a phenomenal young bunch, with passion and integrity. The campaign included a ballsy series of radio ads, again playing on political puns, but with added topical references thrown into the mix. There was a vocal impersonation of firebrand politician Julius Malema, who doubled as a Nando's announcer, and all manner of references to left wings, right wings, demands for change and a request to drop the charges. These matters all had extremely sensitive relevance to the political scene at the time, when Malema was still leader of the youth league for the ruling party, the ANC.

The TV version, which depicted a "Julius" character as a puppet in the hands of a larger puppet master, well, that had the ANC furious.

Politics had always been fertile topical territory for Nando's. We had previously done another fun campaign playing on the words "A and C", which when spoken, are almost indistinguishable from ANC.

Anyway, back during the 2009 elections, we put out another topical campaign that went deep into the politics of the day. Earlier, Jacob Zuma – then deputy president of the country – had faced charges of racketeering and corruption, which were subsequently dropped in mysterious circumstances. It was a situation tailor made for puns about dropping the charges on our chicken combos.

So, we finished the material for the campaign on a Friday. It went live during the weekend. On Monday morning I received a call.

"Is that Sylvester Chauke?"

"Yes, who's speaking?"

"This is Mathews Phosa, treasurer-general of the African National Congress."

"Oh ... Hi, sir."

"I need to see you tomorrow at two o'clock at Luthuli House."

I don't suffer from panic attacks, but, I can tell you, I started getting some symptoms right at that moment. I was being summoned to the national headquarters of the ruling party to account for our satirical advertising campaign.

I first began to understand the impact a brand can have on popular culture when our chicken commercials started having an effect in the very corridors of power! I immediately called Kevin; we had to go to that meeting. At one stage, there was talk about attending the meeting with legal counsel, but in the end, it was just myself and Lara Easthorpe, our brilliant brand manager. I insisted that it would be better that way. I did not want to risk a major war alongside two Jewish lawyers at Luthuli House. Imagine!

We eventually got to meet with Mr Phosa, who is a senior, highly respected ANC member. He seemed shocked to learn that there was a black guy responsible for this campaign! He seemed a little taken aback, but then he went onto the front foot. How dare we cast such aspersions on the ruling party? We should cancel the campaign immediately!

When I responded, I stripped the issues down to their bare essence.

"Sir," I told him. "I'm just a young black boy trying to sell chicken and chips."

I said it with a twinkle in my eye, and I think I hit just the right tone, because Phosa burst out laughing! That tilted the meeting in our favour for a while, and we started getting on like a house on fire. It was going amazingly well. We started laughing with each other and having an incredible, deep conversation. Then he snapped out of it and started demanding we cancel the campaign again. He wasn't having it. I asked him to give me a couple of days. Of course, during those couple of days the ads were all over the internet and right across broadcast media. In typical Nando's style, we responded with a "censored" version that took the mickey of the main ad. Genius but scary!

According to Mr Phosa, the ANC Youth League members were apparently highly upset about the campaign and how it depicted their leader. There were concerns that there might be a boycott and that it might affect business. We were a little worried for my safety at one stage, but our story was soon overtaken by something else on the news cycle. It all blew over, but what has stayed with me about the whole affair was the ability of communication to impact public culture in this way. Nando's always tried to articulate the things that people wanted to say, but didn't have the guts to say in public. We weren't just making things up to get noticed – these were feelings that people had at the time.

To execute campaigns that play on those feelings takes skill, but also courage. The people in the Nando's team were so brave. They were constantly pushing the envelope, along with our incredible partners at the agency. They knew how to make sure the content was relevant, and responded to what was happening using the right tone. It was generally about challenging the status quo, but in a charming way that made people laugh. That last part is an important ingredient – if you can make people laugh, you can get away with a lot! In the end, we kept our tone right on the edge. They got to know us well at the advertising standards authority, where we had to report from time to time to deal with complaints about our campaigns.

In the depths of these stressful episodes, Robbie Brozin used to ask me how I was feeling.

"I feel sick," I would reply. "I feel nervous down to the pit of my stomach."

"If you feel nervous, you're onto something," he replied. "That's when you know you're on the edge. If you don't feel nervous, you're still in the comfort zone, and then it wouldn't mean anything."

At Nando's I gained an appreciation for the art of pushing the limits and skating the edge of what is permissible. Pushing the boundaries is a delicate dance, and an approach that's not going to suit every brand. But some brands are simply upstarts, with a disruptor attitude, and being edgy is part of their DNA. Handling messaging for these brands is incredible, because it challenges your reading of contemporary culture, the attitudes of your market, and the abilities of your creatives to hit just the perfect tone. Tip over into bitter sarcasm or insults, and you can offend people – especially in the already polarised political scene.

"You're not going to make everyone happy," Kevin Utian told me. "But as long as you have more people standing with you than against you, then you're fine."

I might be stealing someone else's brand slogan, and labouring the chicken puns, but Nando's gave me wings. FCB and Ogilvy had reared me. DDB toughened me up, but at Nando's I was engaged in a kind of marketing that allowed me to be my best self. It also put me in the line of fire. Luckily, that Mathews Phosa episode was about as much trouble as you can get into with a satirical ad campaign.

I'm also encouraged that, while some of the work I've done has helped to set certain creative and business standards, we've also made a statement for freedom of expression in our industry. Those Nando's campaigns helped to define what would be acceptable in the marketing space, and how far the power of the ruling party extended. These are not matters to be taken too lightly, especially in a young democracy.

———— • ————

Those particular campaigns ran about a decade ago. Would that kind of campaign fly today? Perhaps not. It seems our people have become that much more intolerant of being offended.

Our people are angry, and there are many reasons for that. This makes the perils of edgy advertising even riskier. Heaven forbid a brand comes out with a tone-deaf or oblivious set of ads that is out of step with the current mood and our values! Retribution can be swift, and not always lawful. In today's more flammable social climate, I sometimes feel so sorry for comedians and satirists who thrive on being on that edge. They have to get their humour just right.

That ANC incident also brought me to people's attention in the broader society. It did wonders for my ongoing process of becoming "micro famous"! From then on, people were interested in meeting me. People wanted to know the people behind the campaign. There were several media interviews and, as national marketing manager, it was often my job to respond on behalf of the company. The CEO referred all queries to me. It was also perfect that I was black!

With my fledgling wings on my back, it was up to me to take the plunge out of the nest and to fly. That takes courage. A raging controversy at the intersection of media, business, politics and freedom of speech – that's serious stuff. It takes some scrambling to deal with it, and you need to be pretty brave. As soon as you fly in from the controversy cyclone and dust yourself off, there will be another crisis and you'll have to head back out and do it all over again. Push the envelope again. Offend the same people who have told you never to do it again. Do it because you believe you're on the side of truth, and that you have a right to use your voice.

Some business challenges require skill, some experience, some empathy, but some require pure courage. Anyone pursuing personal growth and success would do well to remember that. Be brave. Growth takes courage. You'll struggle to make the grade without it. You need courage to face stressful situations. You also require it to venture into those dark, neglected spaces within yourself and to ask yourself some difficult questions. It takes courage to stand up for your values. Coincidentally, it's also one of the values that Nando's values most as an organisation. You've got to have courage to survive.

There will be moments where you will need courage to face internal challenges, to stand up to your boss and fight for an idea you really believe in. That can be even more difficult than facing an external threat. With your colleagues, you have relationships that are so much deeper. Fortunately, our CEO was an edgy guy, so he was on our side.

"Is this the best we can do?" he would ask when I showed him some proofs of our ads. "Can't we push it out a bit more?"

"I'm a bit nervous about this campaign," I might say.

"We can do better," would be his final word.

Kevin is a ballsy, bold gentleman. One of the best CEOs I've worked with. Despite all his experience, he seemed to have no baggage. He was not damaged by any previous reversals of fortune he might have had. He was always courageous and prepared to take risks. He knew we had a strong brand, able to withstand a small overreaction.

"Let's try," he would say. "If it doesn't work, we move on."

When you have a leader like that backing you, you feel ready to take on the world.

That same bravado ran through the entire executive team and the management team. You can't hunt on your own – teamwork is vital. I would be the guy who got to speak on television, which made it look like the whole campaign was my idea. But I was just doing a job, and my colleagues understood that. They made things happen as much as I did, and we were all in the trenches together. I just stuck my head out every now and then to provide commentary.

At Nando's I earned my licence to create. That phase is one of the pillars on which my career has been built. After a while, the company started going through some changes – as all businesses do. Kevin Utian moved on, which left an enormous gap in the company – and in my professional life. In the weeks after he left, it felt like we were mourning a father. For me, Kevin was so many things. He was a springboard I could use to launch myself to greater heights. He helped me go further than I ever would have on my own.

Kevin's departure changed my experience at the company. When that happens, it's natural to start looking around. Realists that they were, my colleagues at Nando's were quite open about discussing career options beyond the company. On a few occasions, I remember presenting a job offer I had received from another company to my boss, Robbie Brozin.

"Are you crazy!" I remember him saying. "That's not the company for you! You can find a better place!"

The subtext was that we relish a challenge. And we related as human beings as much as co-workers. My managers accepted that sooner or later I would probably move on. They just seemed keen to make sure that when I left for new pastures, I was going on to something even better, greater than what Nando's was.

That attitude shows deep generosity of spirit. It's kindness. It's humanity. Robbie had seen many people like me in his career, and he would see many more. But he cared enough to want the best for me in my next job.

———•———

When my next job opportunity arrived, it was at MTV. When I told Robbie I'd got the MTV job, he was thrilled! I moved on with his blessing. Again, I managed to make a change where everyone was satisfied. I had added another precious clutch of magic relationships to my priceless horde, to keep safe and connected as I moved forward. I left Nando's after a wild farewell at the Nando's Central Kitchen, our corporate headquarters in Lorentzville, Joburg.

Robbie made a very generous speech. Paul Appleton, too. They said I had managed to put my stamp on the company culture. Then we got up and danced to Madonna!

I left Nando's knowing that I had made an impact – within the company and through the company. Every year since I left, I've received social calls from people I worked with at that company. I've managed not to cut ties at all. It seems more straightforward staying in touch when you were employees together. Working as an entrepreneur, it can be ugly. Most relationships are beautiful, but, once in a while, a relationship has to be sacrificed.

I'm able to go back and visit colleagues at my former companies because I'm a product of those spaces. We remind each other of our earliest successes. This is especially true if you see your career as a process of accumulating contacts, making friends and growing. A network must expand, as we follow the arc of our career trajectory. We wouldn't want to have 20 acquaintances at one company, then to leave and simply replace those 20 with another 20 acquaintances at the next place! It's more rewarding to save those acquaintances, to keep them with you, and to grow them into a massive group of connections you can have for life.

Every experience is worth putting in your drawer, so to speak. It's worth saving for the future. One of the earliest experiences in my drawer of professional memories is my first-year lecturer from university. She had lectured me back in the nineties, and she popped into the office to say hi and to congratulate me on my progress thus far. I'm happy that we're still in touch, and, on a certain level, I'm proud that she's proud.

40

It's not just about the CV

AT DNA, WE HAD won a campaign for a big client and, as part of the casting process, we put out a call for recent black graduates. We were looking to put together a dedicated group of young people to represent the brand. They would be brand representatives, not influencers in the traditional sense, more like ambassadors who could work with the team in retail stores and activation spaces.

We placed a job ad and, within the first hour, 480 CVs had arrived. By the end of the week, we had 1 500! We ended up with about 8 000 job applications for this handful of brand ambassador positions. It was crazy to think how hungry our people are to get jobs. We made our initial selections and then began our first batch of interviews to select these young people. We formed a panel and set up casting chairs for the interviews. The candidates got to introduce themselves to the panel and explain their skill set. I was disappointed to learn that of the first 100 people we saw, only 15 were good enough to make it to the next stage.

These were all graduates. They each had a university degree, but none of them had done any work in their careers up to that point!

I understand that jobs are hard to come by in this economy, but there are still opportunities to do some good. There are any number of unpaid service opportunities on offer at NGOs, or community groups. You can approach a business about unpaid internships, volunteering or job shadowing. You can build online businesses and social awareness campaigns ... In our case, out of our entire intake, so few of the candidates succeeded in distinguishing themselves from their rivals.

They also seemed to lack self-knowledge. When we asked them direct questions about themselves – their values, their ambitions, their hopes and dreams, it was as if they had never considered them before. For me, these were basics that had been neglected. You need purpose in life, and part of creating that purpose is sincere self-reflection and understanding. You really need to get to know yourself. When you understand what's important to you, you know what you want, and then you can start working out how you want to go out and get it.

Before someone else asks you those questions, you should ask them of yourself. They're important questions to help you understand yourself, and to help others understand you.

——— ·•· ———

I've kept a short list of important questions that I believe recent graduates and applicants should ask themselves when they're looking for work. Knowing the answers to these questions will help you to properly articulate why a company should choose you over anyone else.

What are you good at?

Yes, you've got a degree in marketing and communication. But what are you good at? For me, it's analytics. I'm good at running campaigns and building relationships. I make friends. I love to be with people, and it's one of my strengths. Some call it the soft side of business – which is odd for me. There is an entire universe of possible skills a person can have.

What are *your* strongest attributes? Are you good at putting together presentations? Can you write well? Communicate a strategy? Perhaps you're strong at managing projects or at leading them? Perhaps making sales and securing new business is one of your strengths? I respect people who can take briefs. They can interpret them and make sure they're executed as planned. What is your strength? Knowing that takes self-awareness.

What are you willing to do?

If you're ever lucky enough to arrive at a company as an intern, your answer to this question should be, "Whatever you need". As team members, we are there to help. If we have a healthy service ethic, we should be prepared to do what's required at any time. That includes all kinds of "soft" services, like making sure the water cooler tanks are replaced regularly, organising farewells and, yes, making coffee for your boss! Know what the menu is at your boss's favourite lunch restaurant. Book meeting rooms. Act as a PA for a busy person who needs one. Be ready to serve.

What is happening in the news today?

Whatever sector you enter, it will be operating within a particular social and economic environment. Current affairs is what shapes that environment – locally and internationally. By educating yourself on the business environment and the current affairs that shape it, you can get closer to understanding why executives make the decisions they do. You get to understand your industry better.

If you had a magic wand, and you could do anything, what would you do?

We all need to dream. Dreaming keeps us young. It speaks to possibility. It helps us dare to imagine. Companies like to have dreamers. These are the kinds of people who imagine better worlds. Knowing what you would dearly love to experience also provides you with a personal north star to head towards. It gives you purpose. I believe it's important to have at least one crazy dream. For me – hanging at the ISS (International Space Station) reading a book floating in space is one! Can't wait!

What are your interests?

Here you get to showcase yourself. You might not have a full-time job, but what else have you done? Have you worked at a supermarket? Volunteered with your youth group? Been a shop assistant? Gone on marches? Joined a community group? If our industry interests you, how have you been moving yourself towards a career in this field? If you're hoping to become a brand ambassador, perhaps you've been building a personal brand, with an Instagram account, online business or a video blog. All of these kinds of activities show vision.

———•———

I would never be so bold as to say I planned my career with

complete, meticulous vision. It may look semi-organised in retrospect, but it certainly wasn't all that structured. I do believe that if you have the self-awareness to ask yourself questions about what is important to you, your life gains stability, a sense of direction. Without it, you start to drift. You begin to simply hope for the best instead of working to make it a reality. Life is not so generous that it gives you things for simply hoping. You also have to play your part in actively improving your situation, making the best use of the space on this earth that you've been granted.

We may be touching on something that happens when we move from adolescence into adulthood, which is taking ownership of your own life. This is a crucial life stage. Some of us are blessed to have caring parents and families that have helped us through life. We get sent to school. Then we're at university, and then we get given taxi fare to come to a job interview. At a certain stage, you need to take charge of your own destiny. Work out what you want from life, and then start crafting strategies to get it.

41

Getting my African groove back

MTV WAS A PAN-AFRICAN opportunity. I was no longer going to be playing in the South African market alone. SA makes up only one part of the MTV Africa territory. When I joined as the director of marketing & communication, Nigeria was by far the biggest market, with other significant audiences in Kenya and Ghana. Working at MTV would require me to shift my thinking completely.

FCB had given me a solid foundation, DDB had chiselled me into shape. Nando's had given me wings. But this was a totally different world. My time at MTV taught me to understand the continent, to *love* the continent. I had a South African perspective, but I was determined to be open minded, and to learn as much as I could about how business is done in other countries.

South Africa may be the most developed country on the African continent, but our market is not growing as rapidly as many of our African partners. Parts of the continent are booming, and we're now seeing a shift in emphasis to the other territories. MTV has been working with this perspective for the past 15 years. At MTV, we speak in dollars, the currency of Africa. And there were big dollars being mentioned.

My world expanded. To do my job properly, I needed a completely global perspective. I was constantly flying to meetings in Lagos or Nairobi, or to other MTV markets in Europe and the States. Synchronising our operations here in the EMEA region (Europe, Middle East and Africa), with New York HQ took some planning. We shifted our office hours to 9.30am to 6pm. This meant we could schedule the phone calls to New York for the end of the day, when our US colleagues were just starting work.

Those office hours have stayed with me. Today, the working day at DNA is 9.30am to 6pm. It keeps us plugged into the global schedule. It also means that everybody can drop the kids off at school, or go to gym, and be at work in plenty of time. People need to go to the gym; they need to go shopping. They need to do the personal admin that goes with having a life. Shifting the hours that little bit also means we miss most of the heinous Joburg rush-hour traffic. Calls to clients in New York are scheduled for 4pm, at which point our energy levels are still high. It works.

Everything happens within a context, and the geopolitical context is an important part of that. Living in South Africa can make you insular. When you leave our borders, I've found you gain a perspective on our country as part of a whole, and where we fit into it. We are certainly significant players in Africa, but we're not the only game in town. South Africa is not what the rest of the continent is like. We have some amazing achievements to be proud of here, but we do not have the spirit, the heart, the hardworking hustle, the tech savvy that we find in other African countries. African people are finding African solutions. There are ideas that are changing lives. There's an explosion of technological innovation happening on the continent, and at MTV I was a customer of innovation.

One of the biggest lessons I took from those years was an awe and appreciation for people's resourcefulness. Africans are able to make a lot with nothing. From limited assets, incredible innovation is emerging. People are positive, and they're pushing forward. They seem unstoppable! At MTV, I was fortunate to experience that indomitable spirit. The heart of that African spirit isn't in South Africa. That African spirit lives in West Africa. In East Africa. Down here in the South, we're aware of our African-ness, but we lose touch with it sometimes. We're also a little bit spoiled. We have so many resources at our disposal in terms of communications and connectivity, infrastructure, access to finance and support networks, but still our level of innovation cannot match that of our African sisters and brothers. When we South Africans start to travel across the region more often, perhaps we will learn some of that African resourcefulness and really start to make the most of what we have.

Our infrastructure is unrivalled, yet East African fintech companies are helping to redefine financial systems and telecommunications through mobile phone-based financial services. Other microfinance services allow entrepreneurs to run small businesses, getting loans and billing for services using only a basic feature phone.

If we could marry South Africa's infrastructure with innovation from the rest of the continent, we would be invincible!

My boss at MTV was the company SVP and MD, Alex Okosi. He wanted our content to be nothing less than brilliantly pan-African and amazing at all times. That was a philosophy that was drummed into me, and I fell in love with it. I also got access to some of the most epic parties and events across Africa!

I worked for MTV! I was popping bottles in the most incredible nightclubs. I got to attend the EMAs, to be on the red carpet with the global team. There was little old me from Soweto on the red carpet in Madrid. I was moving with the global players! I started to feel that the world needed to understand our continent, to see our true brilliance.

That became our message. We sent it cascading through our channels. We came in with confidence and pride. No insecurities. We presented our continent to the world in the best possible light, showcasing our talent everywhere. We were representing Africa, and Africa was the future.

With our young population and limitless investment opportunities, Africa is primed for growth. Savvy investors are beginning to wake up to this. Africa has an enormous contribution to make in enriching the global economy and global culture. People like Trevor Noah, Lupita Nyong'o and Black Coffee are already doing us proud as entertainers who wear their African identity comfortably. South African artists like Cassper Nyovest and AKA are building relationships with counterparts in other African cities. We are building a pan-African sound with local flavours. Afrobeat, the irresistible music style out of West Africa, is influencing pop, hip-hop and dance music across the planet.

The world is becoming interested in Africa. Delivering Africa to the world was MTV, or the Viacom Africa network. Content was the game, across multiple channels. The MTV Base channel had a strong music focus, Nickelodeon offered entertainment viewing for children. Then there was VH1 and Comedy Central.

The content had become more varied, but music was key. MTV was also able to play an incredible role in building an African awareness within the continent. We were able to find the grooviest artists, performing in local markets, and to put them on an MTV platform where their work would be amplified across the continent. We were able to find regional stars and introduce them to the larger African entertainment scene. This was not a complex strategy, but it required almost bottomless reserves of passion and energy to execute. It was a completely different level of business. It had to be driven by love.

I was director of marketing and communications for an African company. To do that effectively, I almost had to shed my skin as a South African man, and learn to express the pan-African identity I had almost forgotten was within me. Complicating the process slightly was that we had to do all of this from our offices in Johannesburg, South Africa. We had to constantly be reminding ourselves of that: "Okay, we're in South Africa, but this has to work in Kenya."

We had the analytics to measure what reception our content was having in different areas. We worked to constantly refine our offering, learning what people liked and ensuring that what we put out would resonate with all African people.

The steps to my awakening as an African business person were important. Firstly, I learned that every piece of content or messaging you create should be relatable for everyone on the continent.

Secondly, you have to be a student. To grow, you have to be prepared to learn, and to listen. You can also actively study our shared history and culture. Ask questions, listen to people's answers.

A slight shortcoming of some South Africans in the African context is an arrogance, or a lack of humility. This is an unnecessary barrier. We have much to learn from our African brothers and sisters. An example is the South African idea of "foreigners". We seem obsessed with the idea, to the point of violently attacking the recent arrivals in our country, these new South Africans. It's such a closed-minded limitation – to still be hung up on a set of borders set up by colonial powers in the 19th century in order to divide Africans. When I was in Lagos, I did not feel like a foreigner. It seemed everyone was accustomed to welcoming people from all over the continent and engaging warmly.

South Africans can also be limited by our understanding of value. We might overlook the innovation and the opportunity in other countries because the systems of assessment we use do not account for that value. Baldly put, we see anything from the rest of Africa as inferior, or "other". We might describe trade with other parts of our region as "business with Africa", as if Africa doesn't include South Africa. South Africans struggle to see themselves as African in anything beyond a geographical way.

At the same time, all African cities have incredible, almost insurmountable challenges. The traffic situation in Lagos is diabolical. It's crazy, it's crowded and it takes you absolute hours to get anywhere. So you can't dismiss the value of working infrastructure. Facilities as basic as roads, telecoms and electricity networks that (largely) function, give South Africa a significant advantage. But until we embrace our pan-African identity, we are short-changing ourselves. We are minimising our experiences.

As South Africans, our perspectives limit us. We are prepared to jump on a plane to Dubai at the drop of a hat, but we might never quite get around to visiting places like Zambia, or Mozambique. Perhaps because of the history of the continent, our minds have been trained to isolate ourselves from our neighbours. I hope we can change that.

211

I believe that embracing our African identity can have spiritual, financial and practical benefits. Once you start to travel, you learn to be resourceful, because life is tougher. Man, everything's harder up there.

I love the people of Lagos, and the experiences I've had there. I love the energy of the city. But when it rains, the traffic just stops moving. The result is that you become reluctant to leave a meeting because you might become trapped in an all-day gridlock and never make it to the airport tomorrow. You just don't know!

We were always on a tight schedule, and I would spend my entire time in Lagos keenly aware that I had a flight to catch or I had a hotel room to get to. The uncertainty and the massive amounts of time and money it costs can become frustrating, but the passion, the creativity and the incredible energy make it more than bearable. Africans are such inspiring people.

———•———

When you see the rest of Africa, you start to recognise the African elements of your own culture. You realise that, actually, we *are* African. We *do* have that African groove. We just need to get our groove back. The way we speak when we engage with our people – there is an emotiveness. There's a connection. That's African. The way we negotiate when do business. How we draw things out, our love of protocol.

The way of doing business in Africa is severely underplayed, and deserving of further study. There is an American approach, aggressive and brash. Then an Asian way, with a strong focus on group interests. In the African business approach, there's an understanding that the final agreement must work for everyone. The benefits must be mutual. We're not here to try to screw each other as badly as we can! African business can be more collaborative. It's an authentically human way of interacting. Like many of our cultural traditions, African business can also involve a long period of simply getting to know each other.

Getting straight down to business is overly hasty. It's polite to enquire about each other's lives, our families. To share what we have in common. Such formalities help us understand each other better and assist in the negotiations to come.

It's beautiful, and it's African.

42

I was never ready

I WAS AT MTV through 2010, when South Africa hosted the FIFA World Cup. The next year, DNA started.

Many prospective entrepreneurs ask me when I knew I was ready to start a business. I reply that I wasn't ready. And I would never have been ready. I could have waited another decade, and I still would not have been ready. I would not have been ready, because there are certain things you need to know to start a business, but you can only learn them by *starting a business*.

The best way to learn about business is to be in businesses. That said, it helps to gain some industry knowledge before launching your own start-up. Working for several years will also give you the chance to build those precious networks. That network that you also think of as your circle of friends? One day, that network will be a source of business.

It would be incredibly difficult to start a business right after school, because you have none of the support networks in place, few of the skills and no access to finance. Entrepreneurship is often touted as the solution to our country's jobs crisis, but it can only work if it goes together with effective skills transfer. You need *a tonne* of skills to run a business. I built up more than a decade of skills in my field before I tried to run my own business. I still ended up pretty much begging to get out of it because it's so complicated! Luckily, no one would let me stop, and, here we are, still in business.

Entrepreneurship is challenging on an almost ludicrous level. It takes over your life. It sends you on a screaming amusement-park ride of emotions every day. You can move from a blissful love-bombing session with a happy client, to two hours of getting shat on relentlessly. It's tough being an entrepreneur, I'm not going to lie. But it's magical.

I was equipped to become an entrepreneur through my time as a salary-earning professional in the marketing industry. It gave me a point of reference, a framework of how my industry works. An understanding of the systems in place in a large organisation.

You can call it paying your dues if you like, but running a business in a competitive sector requires a firm foundation. It's perfectly acceptable to aspire to drive a Bentley one day. Along your way to earning it, you're going to be judged on how you do your work. To earn a Bentley, your work needs to be of Bentley quality. It's awesome to celebrate yourself on Instagram, but you need to be working as well, making those wins that are worth celebrating.

We can't all be entrepreneurs, but we also can't all be employees. We need entrepreneurs to create the businesses to hire the employees! I have friends who are working professionals, who tell me they could never do what I do. They see that I carry stresses with me concerning every part of my business.

I worry about our income, our expenses, our performance this quarter, staffing issues ... An employed director of a multinational company might stress about the targets their division needs to meet, but they don't have to also worry about people's salaries and the computers the company needs to buy or the paper wastage ... These are operational fundamentals that will be familiar to anyone running a business.

Running your own company is not for everyone. It requires a particular kind of patience and grit. But it doesn't make you any less of a person if that's not your space. The world is full of inspirational people working as staff, managers or independent suppliers. Working in a large global corporation can be massively fulfilling.

Starting a business is a different challenge. For those suited to the lifestyle, it can be hellish, but it does become more bearable with time. I have a sense that I would have *had* to do this at some stage. My career path would have demanded it. If I had not started this business, I would have been left wondering what could have been.

At first, I never ever saw myself as an entrepreneur. I thought I would take the corporate route and end up being a CMO, or a senior executive at a company like MTN. As it turns out, that was not to be.

There is no single path to success. We must all find our own. But of all things, I didn't want to become an entrepreneur. It all sounded a little too complex and cumbersome. Then, along the way, something about me changed. I had gained the incredible opportunity to work with MTV across Africa, but I already had a feeling inside myself, wondering what was next.

Many years earlier, just before I had joined Nando's, I had registered a company. I had a thought about perhaps doing something on the side. My idea was for something not directly related to the work I was doing, something to do with solving problems. That business idea simmered for a while. Nando's had taught me creativity and MTV was in the broadcasting communication field. There was the gem of an idea around providing an interesting combination of services.

I saw that many of the fields I had become skilled in could be brought together in a new way. As I moved into the boardroom space and began to have conversations with clients, I began to identify a gap. There were many brands that needed the right kind of treatment to bring them closer to meeting their goals.

The original concept for DNA was for us to operate as brand doctors. If a client brand was not doing well, losing shape, we would propose a complete solution. I soon understood that a brand doesn't need to be doing badly for it to be worthy of good advice. That vision evolved to what we are today – a marketing and brand communications consultancy for brands with an unstoppable hunger for greatness, committed to a re-imagined and inspired continent of Africa.

In ten years' time, DNA will be something different. We are becoming, but whatever we become, we will remain in the business of solving brand problems.

43

Now is my time

MTV IS ONE OF those fast-paced businesses where you can gain the experience in two years that most people will only accumulate in ten. The number of campaigns we launched, across so many markets, outstripped even what I had been doing at Nando's. Many brands might have one big campaign per year, with perhaps three major components. At MTV, we were launching something every six weeks. Always working, always growing.

That growth has continued. As an alumnus of the company, I was invited back to speak at MTV's year-end function recently. The business is almost three times as big as when I left. It has constantly been expanding. Alex has built a phenomenal operation.

When you're in an environment and you understand the vision for the business – say a vision to elevate the African continent –

you're part of that vision. A few years later, you might look back and realise you were pioneers in the space, pioneers in the area of African music, African music videos, and pioneers in the area of African content, marketing the continent to the world. The rest of the world will only realise how innovative you are once you start achieving success.

The only way to know which idea to choose is to embrace that which speaks to you. Find a company whose ideas chime with yours, with the same values you love. Then dedicate yourself to helping them. Learn from them.

Many companies don't offer such opportunities. It's such a privilege and opportunity to learn. People pay a lot of money to learn.

———•———

When I arrived at MTV, I was coming from Nando's, a great space, with my confidence sky high and knowing what I was capable of. I was close to being the finished article. On my first day at MTV, I started making changes. That was how sure of myself I was. If you're younger, and you find yourself in a similar situation, you might want to be more circumspect. Learn from your company and start imagining what you can do with your knowledge.

———•———

I never saw myself as an entrepreneur, but I was highly entrepreneurial in my methods. I came from the agency world, where we are constantly pitching for business. That makes you deeply aware of the business principles at work. You need to get new work in, so you can do the work, and then bill for it. Then you need to find more work. I could never really separate the idea of working for a company from the need to make it profitable. I only understood later that this helped me become a business person.

It also taught me to love business. You are chasing income, tripping on the adrenaline rush that comes from pitching ideas. Even though MTV was a recognisable brand, we still had to sell ourselves. We had to go to even bigger brands, like MTN, and try to get millions of dollars out of them. It's a big deal, and we were doing it. That's entrepreneurship right there.

Luckily, I never expected that leaving MTV to start my own thing was going to mean having to work harder. I was already working like a beast – 16-hour days were standard. That wasn't work policy, but personal choice, and part of a culture of getting the problem solved. It was also fun. We got to understand some of the world's biggest problems from the inside out – everything from war to pollution. And then we tried to solve them. We were hustling, but, in the hustling, we were building something. Under Alex's leadership, I was fired up!

I knew that the biggest obstacle in starting my own business wouldn't be longer work hours. It was more of a financial question. As a salary earner, you know that you have a guaranteed monthly income. As an entrepreneur, there are no guarantees. Some months you can literally earn nothing, and still have massive bills to pay. Going out on your own changes things on an emotional level.

Entrepreneurial thinking is vital if you want to make it in the world in any capacity. Ultimately, it's about looking at a problem, finding a solution and making your money off that. Agencies are a good entrepreneurial training ground, because each division or department runs as a business. As a client-service person, or a strategist, you're aware of how you can price your services, drive your margin and minimise wastage to ensure your department is profitable and that you meet your targets.

When you're coming off a system like that, you soon learn what the score is. As an agency "graduate", I'm lucky to have worked for companies that embrace entrepreneurial thinking.

I learned many amazing tricks of how to ensure profitability while working at agencies. That empowerment didn't just go as far as decision-making and confidence. I was empowered to help run the business.

Employees who think like business owners make better employees. Once a quarter, I stand up in front of our team and present our business position. That is scary for some, but it's real. If the reality of our financial position scares you, you're better off knowing about it. It also helps my colleagues to contextualise their own contribution to our performance. Every line item is revealed, whether it's coffee or the internet line. We get to see where it all fits in, and how we can make a difference. It's also a great opportunity for me to speak to the team. I get to account for the various decisions that we're making, and what purposes they serve. How much money have we made? I try to manage the process as honestly and frankly as possible. Some find it harrowing. Sometimes the understanding is that if the business loses a client then we're going to lose people. Luckily, it's never come to that.

We've never had to lose people, because our strategy has always been to diversify our revenue streams. We can lose two clients, and still be able to redeploy people and remain profitable. We can still provide medical aid and all associated benefits for all our staff. I see that as part of our responsibility. I have a responsibility to the people that I lead. If they fall and hurt themselves, they need to go to hospital. We insource our people. We have no one freelancing.

My understanding has always been that I'm building a business for the future. That means I can't wake up after ten years and introduce a new system of operating. We introduced best practice when we were younger. As we've grown, it's become part of what we do.

That's not to say it's not challenging working here. For everyone, there's a lot of expectation around what you can become or what you need to do. We're trying to open minds to what people's possibilities are beyond their immediate role as a social media community manager, or whatever it might be. We encourage strategic thinking. We encourage our people to get involved with the business. To do that, we need all our people to see the numbers. If someone wants to become a leader of the future, they need to be interested in how businesses run. You can't just sit in a corner and get on with your work.

44

The Tao of DNA

At DNA, if you take a peek into the kitchen, you'll find water, juice, bread, milk and jam ... You can get that energy to help you do your work if you need to. If we can make things easier, we do. Sometimes that is taken for granted, though. If our company is someone's first formal job, they might think this is simply the way things are done in the workplace. In fact, our facilities are better than most other work environments. But the social contract is this: these are best-of-breed working conditions, for which we expect best-of-breed performance.

I am a black leader with a predominantly black staff – an all-black staff, at the moment! I have taken a huge responsibility for all of it. Some of us get a bit lost in the euphoria of all of this, without really understanding the responsibility we have. This needs an occasional reinforcement. We manage our people actively, with our human resources staff.

Managing this set-up of ours takes constant, full-time work.

Young staff can work hard, but they can also be demanding. I wouldn't say entitled, but we do sometimes get complaints when staff receive a 13-inch MacBook, instead of a 15-inch one! Those kinds of expectations can make you feel unappreciated, but then I remind myself that this is exactly what I've been trying to achieve: making excellence the norm. We deserve the best, and we must always expect it. But not everyone needs a 15-inch MacBook.

Managing people can be exhausting, and it requires specialised skills. I have three dedicated HR professionals to manage staff development and recruitment. For many years, I had to carry that by myself. I'm thrilled to have help, but I am also always working to improve my abilities in that regard.

There's an emotional component to management too. I work with a business coach, who has helped me deal with the emotional challenges of managing a large group of people. Leading a team, the issues you have to deal with never stop coming. I suffered greatly under the pressure and soon learned that I needed to have one-on-one time with my coach. I needed to have a safe space where I could be vulnerable, outside of my relationships with my partner and my bestie. That kind of "check in" is critical!

Through all of that, we are pushing the work. The work, the ideas, the solutions are the focus, but you have to also manage a few egos. I encourage my team to try to understand each other, so we can share the work of carrying our company forward. We help everyone understand by being as open as we can, sharing financial updates, so everyone can understand the context each of their colleagues is working from.

The benefits of this approach surface in interesting ways. When we were planning our end-of-year office party, people were coming forward with some incredibly passionate efficiency improvements.

For a while, it became a tradition for us to stay at the African Pride Hotel in Melrose Arch as part of our end-of-year bash. We would check everyone in during the afternoon. Then we would have a photo shoot with the team, followed by a town hall meeting where we present everyone with goodies and look back at the year. Then it gets lit! We celebrate until all hours of the morning, sleep late and then say goodbye in the afternoon.

Running a business remains challenging. I find myself exhausted a lot of the time. We are still a young company, trying to figure it out. But we've built a way of doing things, and we have a long way to go. We create the most pleasant working conditions we can. We pay the best salaries our business can support. I want the best for my people, so that they can give me their best work. I try to be absolutely fair, and, because of that, I'm able to sleep peacefully at night.

"To whom much is given, much is expected," it says in the Book of Luke in the Bible, and that is the principle at work in our agency.

I come from companies where we were well taken care of. In a sense, I'm now paying it forward in my own business. I was treated well, so I try to treat *my* people well. It's what I was taught. We try to be caring in word and deed. In a caring company, managers treat their people with respect in every way – through their benefits and through their interactions. At all the agencies and the companies I've worked at, that was a constant – the authentic, human love.

"What's happening in your life?"

"My child's starting a new school and I'm slightly anxious."

"Oh, I know! It can be a bit difficult at first. But she'll be fine. Good luck with that, my friend."

These kinds of conversations take a few seconds, but they can make a lifetime of difference. They show that we care about each other. In a work environment, speaking to your colleagues in this way shows that it's not *only* about the work. We're all doing our best work. But it's the warm care, the humanity, that keeps us going.

45

This is living

THE LOVE I WAS shown by my colleagues in my career has led me to try to do the same with my team. When I was working for Klasie Wessels at FCB, he would show such faith in me. One December, his family went away to Namibia and he asked me to house-sit for him. There was 20-year-old me, in his palatial home! They even filled up the fridge for me. They said I could invite a few friends over ... I had a week of living like a king!

Asking a kid as young as I was to house-sit for you – that takes a level of trust. But that gesture also had everything to do with giving me an experience that would shake me. Seeing how the privileged people live showed me that I was also starting to move in those circles, and that I was moving forward. It also gave me something to aim for. This was a lifestyle to aspire to! Inviting someone into your home in whatever context is so generous.

Another of my learnings from my mentors has been the value of experiences. As a young person who doesn't come from much, it's natural to spend your first few pay cheques on acquiring possessions. You need them, after all. You need to buy couches; you need appliances; you've got to have a nice painting in the lounge. You're building your nest! But you can't keep collecting things forever. There's only so much space in your house. You can only wear one set of clothes at a time.

It was one of my earliest mentors who told me, "Every time we give you a raise, or you get a bonus, you seem to go out and buy more items. Have you thought about experiencing things more?"

I was so young at the time that I didn't quite grasp what he was getting at. He elected to show me what he meant. He would take me out for dinner and lunch, share a bottle of wine at a great restaurant … He began demonstrating the value of a shared experience.

"I understand what you're trying to show me," I eventually said. "I'll start to focus on experiences once I've finished collecting things."

"You'll never finish collecting things," he replied. "You need to understand what is important to you: things or experiences …"

When I received my next bonus, it came with an air ticket.

"You can fly anywhere in the world," I was told. "Just let us know where you want to go. Then you must go and experience something."

That was how I got to see Paris for the first time. It was an experience that my boss gave me. He taught me the value of travel, the value of taking time out and enjoying the rich experiences life offers.

At Nando's, I went through a stage where I was working quite hard, putting in some weekends and late nights. My boss, Paul Appleton, chose to reward me. He arrived on set one day carrying a little bag. The bag contained several CDs and another R1 000 in vouchers for the music store.

"I know you love music," he said. "I just wanted to show I appreciate how hard you've been working. I just want to say thank you."

———•———

Having gone through that, and having been made to feel so special, how could I keep it for myself? Today, if there's an international trip on the cards for our agency, I will generally travel with someone else from the team. It's always good to share an experience. Last year we won an international award. I travelled to the ceremony in Rome with Cedrick, Obakeng, Vincent and Kutloano just to share the experience and for inspiration.

Their excitement was contagious! It rekindled my love for sharing all over again. We ended up at the Vatican, in St Mark's Square, admiring the Sistine Chapel ... Who would have thought? Who would have thought that a bunch of kids from the township would make it to Rome, onto the world stage!

To travel on business as a young person, to experience something that is life-changing, is incredibly powerful. It's way better than a bonus, sometimes. In business, it can earn you staff loyalty that no raise or performance bonus can match.

It doesn't happen so often in business today. But I strive to replicate for others the kind of experiences that I have been blessed with, and to start cultivating the kind of deep relationships that I still have with the people I've worked with in the past.

46

The courage to self-actualise

My MTV CAREER WAS flying, but I kept being reminded of the company I had registered those few years before. At the time, I had thought I might become a certain type of entrepreneur. I would keep working in my job, and write some strategies for clients on the side, just to make some money over the weekend. For a long time, I had not been able to take any more of a risk than that. Because of my family duties, I felt it would have been irresponsible to risk it all on a full-time business venture. I thought my people were still relying on me.

However, what had happened over the years of my contributing to my family is that it had become easier. I was earning more. My sisters were starting to contribute. I was now able to juggle all my expenses successfully. That was enough for the inspiration to start taking root. And I was working in an inspirational place. MTV inspired an awakening, an enlightenment within me. I started to think bigger, higher, further.

From time to time, someone would ask me to write a strategy for them, I'd do it and they would be happy. Then someone else would ask me for another one. I thought, okay, let me start charging properly. Then I realised that if I could do three of those strategies a month, I would almost be able to live off that. It was an interesting thought. I decided to start drawing on that incredible network of mine, just to check what was possible. If I could confirm the support of a few individuals, I might be able to take the leap. My first port of call was Robbie Brozin at Nando's.

"Robbie," I told him, "I'm thinking of starting something."

"If you do start something," he replied, "I can definitely give you a project or two. Something worth the odd ten grand here or there …"

That was a yes! That was one in the bag. The next person I would approach would be my boss at the time, Alex Okosi from MTV. This is not necessarily part of the entrepreneur's handbook – asking your boss to support you if you resign – but funnily enough, it worked for me. When I told Alex about it, he said he'd also be happy to work with me on a few projects. We had a good working connection as far as visualising ideas.

"What are you going to do?" he asked.

I outlined my idea for my new agency, and he immediately gave me his blessing. I had another supporter on board! After that, I knew I was going to be able to afford petrol money, and to pay my bond. When I eventually did resign, I had a cushion for the first few months. My few early clients allowed me to support myself comfortably from the start of my entrepreneurial career. My first significant clients were both former employers of mine – testament to the value of keeping a healthy network of business mentors and friends.

It was comforting to know that I wasn't bungee jumping into

business without any support. Having a history with so many great brands was also a great help. When I first began going to see people and pitching my services, it was invaluable to be able to list my previous employers and to see potential clients relax when they hear my credentials. Track record is precious in the marketing industry, and when your shiny new brand has no history to speak of, your time with recognised agencies and established brands can convince clients to take a chance on you.

Even though no one could take my work experience away from me, it was still character building to start going into meetings on the strength of my own ability, where previously I had always been representing a bigger company.

"I am not the company I work for," I would tell myself. "But I am amazing. I can do whatever's required."

It was a challenging time, no doubt. But then we secured another client – DSTV. That was a good opportunity to showcase what we could do. Having the country's biggest satellite TV network on your books helps to win more clients, and from there, we started gaining some momentum.

I decided to diversify by buying a share in a small below-the-line agency. They weren't glamorous, but they had some stable clients and were busy. This allowed me the breathing space to put more effort into building DNA, which was barely profitable at that time. Times were tight, but not once did I regret going out on my own. I felt like I was moving. I could see where I was going, and it excited me. I paid no attention to naysayers – and there were a few.

———— ◆ ————

Entrepreneurship is like walking the earth all alone. You can get advice and support, but you alone are taking the risk, and you are the only person standing between success and failure.

Friends don't understand, parents don't get it. No one gets it.

"How could you quit that job at MTV?" I would get asked. "Everyone wants that job. Why did you leave?"

But my vision was clear. This was the next stage of my journey. It was what I needed to do, an experience I needed in my life. My telling of it makes starting a business sound quite romantic, but the reality is quite prosaic. In your head you have this grand idea, but realistically, you've got nothing!

I was blessed in that I didn't need to start my business from home, as many young entrepreneurs have to do. Two young entrepreneurs running a TV production house, Nelisa and Tongai, allowed me to rent some space in their office in the TBWA building. I had done some business with them before, and they had no issues with me paying them a small rent to have a desk and access to their meeting rooms and business facilities. It was a form of co-working, but that is how I grew my business, hiring my first two staff members. I was fortunately able to skip the experience of running a start-up from my bedroom. That's so not me!

I was serious, and I wanted to be in a serious environment, surrounded by like-minded professionals. The offices were in Sandton – the heart of South Africa's financial district. Even though I was renting a few desks and a share of a boardroom for hardly anything, I was able to establish myself in the "richest square mile in Africa". That makes a difference, and also ensured that anyone coming to meet with me would take me seriously. The landline also told people – even if only subconsciously – that mine was a business of consequence. I came from a brand world. I understood the importance of such messaging.

For me, it was also crucial that I have an office to "go to" in the morning. I like to wake up in the morning and go to work. The morning ritual of rising at a specific time, showering, making coffee and dressing for work is important; it gets me in the right frame of mind to start doing business. Even today, when I can easily work from home, I seldom do. I might do some reading at home, but my dogs start fussing with me – and even though I love them, it just doesn't feel like business to me. If I have some important work to do over a weekend, and I need to focus, I will rather come in to the office and do it properly. I have no aversion to working long days on weekends, but I make sure that if I've crushed a big day of work, I go out and celebrate my successes with a great dinner or a show. I know the importance of keeping that balance. It's a bit of a "work hard, play hard" thing, I guess. It's always been my method.

Much as many business people would wish it, you can't have it all. You can't burn the candle at both ends. You also need to reward yourself. If I come into the office on a weekend, I might set myself a goal of finishing a strategy document by 10pm, then call my bestie and say, "We're going out!"

That gives me something to look forward to. I might have sacrificed a day, but in the evening, I'll take two or three hours out and enjoy myself. When I relax after a long day, it feels like I come back to myself.

———◆———

When I was starting out as an entrepreneur, I also had an interest in a BTL production company based in a nondescript part of Randburg. I was like: "Guys, I'm sorry. If you want to be big and fabulous, you cannot be operating from Randburg. Can you even deliver great work with this vibe?"

For the brands they were hoping to get, they just did not look the part. They had some strong clients in the fast-moving consumer goods space, but I felt they would struggle to land bigger clients until they began to think bigger and to position themselves alongside those aspirational clients.

Then an opportunity came. The lease was expiring. I encouraged the leadership to find new premises in a more dynamic part of town. I suggested the Design Quarter in Fourways – near the Johannesburg agency district.

My business partners weren't too keen at the time, but I was smitten. Today, Design Quarter is home to the DNA offices.

At that stage, I still had my little entity in my shared office space, which is where I met Ivan, who would eventually design the DNA offices. The minute we took the leap and moved to the Design Quarter, our fortunes improved. It became clear what a difference an aspirational attitude can make. Business picked up quickly for DNA. Having our own space crystallised the DNA idea. Was it about image? Positioning? I would rather call it clarity. Clarity about what I wanted my business to be, what it should stand for. I had to decide what I wanted to create. Was it a small agency or something substantial? In our minds, we wanted to be more, so we positioned ourselves that way from the start. To this day, that's how we operate. It's how we show up. When a client walks into our agency, there's immediately an expectation. They feel like they're hanging with the best, people who can make things happen. The best clients want to work with people who care about themselves and what they do.

At DNA, we don't sell an image. Instead, our image reflects our clarity of purpose. The choices you make as a brand are intimately tied up with your choices as an entrepreneur. I knew that I needed to make some of those choices if I was going to manifest what I wanted. I'm such a believer in visualisation. From the early days of my business, I have always been able to picture what the next stage of our development would look like. By the time it happened, I had played it through in my mind dozens of times.

In the early days, a devil's advocate would have said that our offices were extravagant. That we couldn't afford them.

We didn't yet have many clients, and we were already wasting money. I'm not advocating that you start spending money you don't have. But when you do start earning money, you need to be clear about what you spend it on. You need the clarity to know what your priorities are and to budget accordingly.

You can also create a professional look and feel without spending a lot of money. The same approach of inexpensive innovation that I use in my fashion approach can also work in interior design. We value ourselves but we don't spend what we don't have. Where we sit has to reflect us. This is a business that is growing.

It's become the norm to herd people into cubicle farms, but that can't produce the best work. An aesthetic has a direct impact on performance, but it's often overlooked. It's very real. It's scary how real it is. At DNA, we're doing what makes us happy, what makes me feel more connected to what's happening.

It's easier to recognise the humanity in your colleagues when everyone's in a happy, positive space. Unhappy people retreat into a more impersonal mindset, and that is the kiss of death. When you start looking at people as just employees and numbers and spaces, the human element starts to die. It's harder to keep that humanity alive in the tough times, and that's when people decide to start cutting headcount.

At our company, during the tough times, we try to make whatever decisions we need to keep the jobs. I can only speak as a young entrepreneur who hasn't seen that much, or had to suffer through such tough times. By the time I've been running the business for 20 years, I would have a better understanding of the business cycle. I hope to continue learning.

You don't prioritise champagne over operational excellence. You cannot make money only to spend it all. You've got to spend what you can afford and make that work for you ... With your values intact. What seem to be extravagances can be investments. They can lead your business to make you money in new ways, they can build morale and spirit, help people work together.

There are some learnings that lie ahead for me. I'm nervous, but cautiously optimistic and I know that if I'm going to be a great leader in the future, I also need to go through some things. Luckily, I have a set of values that I've inherited from my family, my community and my faith. Those values help me stay in touch with why we're doing this.

47

A vision of the next reality

As black people in South Africa, we have a lot against us. That said, we are building a network of a new crop of young leaders who are determined to change things for the better. We often have to contend highly untransformed industries and we have to stay strong in the mission. With mentors around us guiding and supporting our growth, CEOs and CMOs who are committed to real transformation, friends who truly care, partners who support us, and the divine hand that facilitates it all, we are so going to get there!

I had a vision of an upscale agency and, through the grace of God, I've been able to make it a reality. What could be our next reality?

As I navigate this space, I realise that South Africans are not really good at penetrating the mainstream from the periphery. We are actually in a position to start building a brand communications space that is uniquely our own, in our own "language". Instead, we seem content to take what Europe and the US are doing, and to just localise it.

I love reading the wisdom of international ad-industry titans. A few months ago I posted a quote by David Ogilvy on my Instagram account. Ogilvy, the Saatchi brothers, Bill Bernbach, who founded DDB – they lived every marketing challenge we face, and they have incredible advice to share about it. But I think the industry is ready to have Africans making contributions to the world of brand communication. We're not doing it yet. We're not seeing the African way being demonstrated in how brands are communicating around the world. But the world is starting to look at us now and there's a shift, you can see that people are interested in what we have to offer. That can help shape the future of our industry.

My vision, for myself and my team, is to have a bigger stake in the economy of brand communication – whatever form that might take. To do that, we've got to develop the theories that are going to change things. We've got to have the hypotheses that are interesting, and which can be useful. In the next 100 years, I would like to see us being lifted up into spaces where we can shape the way communications happens. I would like university students to learn about the African creatives, and the business people who have elevated the industry, with theoretical contributions and insights. We need to do what's necessary to make Africa – and South Africa – a core part of the brand communication world.

Our methods of working needn't all come from American or British experiences. What is a uniquely South African insight that can drive the world? We're talking to a global human consumer, and Africans are brilliantly equipped to talk to them. We straddle developed and developing worlds, we are multilingual, multicultural, multitalented … We can add our perspectives to the mainstream. That's an element to the brand-communication universe that we are busy fixing. The other bit is how business is done.

When people walk into the DNA office, they tell me it feels like they could be anywhere in the world. When I ask them why that is, they tell me it's the energy, the people and their thinking. That's good. That's an interesting, start. From here, I want to experiment with what business can be like.

A few months ago, I was invited to Harvard. A few of us "millennials" were invited to talk about the future of business, and I delivered a paper. That was great! For an African professional to be celebrated and talked about, that shows we're starting to find our voice.

Setbacks, betrayal and disappointment that I've experienced will also shape my vision of the future. Each time I've had a setback, it forces me to ask myself whether I've made a bad decision. Often, I have! I have a bank of such epiphanies, but there is a comfort in that I learn from those bad decisions and overcome those setbacks. Still, those are some highly emotional moments. I get exhausted. But I also get a wonderful sense of achievement that I can just grow.

It's a challenge. A slightly odd question that people ask me is "What is the worst that can happen when you're running a business?" I've been asked that more than once, which tells me that often it's fear that keeps people from taking risks. But the question does make me think. What is it? What is the worst that can happen? You lose your money, and you're back where you started? You could have some really difficult, complicated experiences that challenge you to your very core and force you to dig deep and reach new levels of motivation?

That could happen, and you could even fail. But that is a precious, incredible opportunity, to have yourself tested like that. When I've faced adversity, I have opened myself up to the

240

thing and I have learned.

Mainly, what I have learned is this: No matter what you do, it's not about you.

It's about what you do for people. To do that effectively, you've got to be aware, and you've got to stay woke. Don't ever assume things. Take every listening opportunity. Listen with your ears, your eyes, your heart and your entire being. Listen to what people tell you, feel them and understand them. They are like you, so the better you know yourself, the better you will know them. Understand yourself, understand what is important to you. At the deepest level. What is important to you? Those are your values, and those things are important to others too. That is how you get to know people.

When you know people, you can help them solve their problems. And helping people solve their problems – serving them and making their lives better – is one of the greatest privileges in life.